Dimensions
of the
Environmental Crisis

John A. Day
Professor of Physics
and Environmental Studies
Linfield College

Frederic F. Fost
Professor and
Head of the
Department of Philosophy
Linfield College

Peter Rose

John Wiley & Sons, Inc.

New York • London • Sydney • Toronto

Library of Congress Catalogue Card Number: 76-166314

ISBN 0-471-19993-1 (cloth)   ISBN 0-471-19994-X (paper)

Printed in the United States of America.

10 9 8 7 6 5 4 3 2 1

Dimensions
of the
Environmental Crisis

Preface

That man has the ability to reverse the present trend of environmental decay is not in doubt. The question is, "How long will it take him to make the necessary adjustments in his outlook?" Whether we are talking about controlling pollution or population, managing food or energy resources, or preserving the natural beauty of wilderness areas, no effective and lasting solution is possible unless there are fundamental changes in human attitudes and behavior. Above all, we must learn that the phrase *Man and his Environment* does not refer to two separate entities that can be considered in isolation from one another, but to a single complex ecosystem—spaceship earth.

The principal purpose of this book is to emphasize the many interrelated dimensions of the environmental crisis, and hence to demonstrate that a permanent solution can come only through an interdisciplinary approach in which knowledge of the humanities is integrated with that of science and technology. Accordingly, rather than attempting to deal with every aspect of the crisis, we explore the basic nature of the problems and their solutions. The desire to be realistic and constructive has been an important restraint upon the selection of material.

The first section (Cultural Background) deals with the deep-rooted cultural factors which have contributed to the environmental crisis and which have determined many of our present-day attitudes toward the environment. Section 2 (Global Aspect) illustrates and emphasizes the fact that serious environmental problems constitute a worldwide phenomenon that recognizes neither geographical nor political frontiers. In Section 3 (Key Elements: Population and

Energy) we consider the conflicts of values and ethical dilemmas underlying two of the most fundamental problem areas. The final section of the book (Basic Approaches to the Solution) takes a hard look at the practical aspects of solving the environmental crisis, including the role of universities, the legal and political implications, and the need for novel interdisciplinary research.

To help bring the issues into sharper focus, each section is introduced by a series of thought-provoking questions. The first question in each series identifies the major purpose of the section as a whole. The remainder are some of the principal questions considered by the articles in the section. Illustrations and quotations have been included primarily to stimulate the reader's imagination and to heighten his sense of involvement.

The idea for this book emerged from an interdisciplinary course—*Freedom and Authority*—established at Linfield College in 1961 to provide in-depth study and discussion of the fundamental issues involved in vital public topics. A recent subject of the course has been *Dimensions of the Environmental Crisis.*

This text is suitable for a broad reading audience, including college students, professional people, and all those who are concerned in finding realistic solutions to our environmental problems. It is suitable for both science and humanities students, and will be particularly valuable to those general science courses now being organized around environmental science.

We hope that the reader will obtain from this book a broader perspective and a deeper insight with respect to the environmental crisis, and will be encouraged to make a personal contribution toward solving these most crucial problems of our time.

Linfield College   *John A. Day*
McMinnville, Oregon   *Frederic F. Fost*
July 1971   *Peter Rose*

Contents

Dimensions
of the
Environmental Crisis

Cultural Background

HOW MUCH HAS OUR CULTURAL BACKGROUND CONTRIBUTED TO THE PRESENT ENVIRONMENTAL CRISIS?

To what extent is religious tradition responsible for our attitudes toward the environment and the subhuman world?

Could we solve our environmental problems by reverting to a primitive view of man's relationship with nature?

Must we choose between returning to a more primitive way of life and accepting a completely man-made environment?

If we are to avoid extreme solutions, in what essential ways must we change our attitudes toward ourselves and the world around us?

In our explosively changing world it is no longer sufficient to live with philosophies or religions simply handed down from an older generation. We must take up a vital, flexible, and ever-evolving concern about the nature and purpose of man, and about what constitutes a good life and a good society . . . .

Rather than simply fight for the preservation of the old things that are good, we must plan creatively also to shape the new. We must commit ourselves to dare to build the world we want, knowing that it is possible if we but demand it—if we use intelligently all the potent forces of science, the arts and the humanities that are at our disposal.

To be what we can be, we must be unafraid to place ourselves, our ways of life, our economic systems, in the microscope of science; and we must have the courage to put into practice the findings that come out, no matter how hard they hit at the patterns of our folkways. To be what we can be, we must first and foremost know what we want to be.

Walter Orr Roberts

The Cultural Basis
for Our
Environmental Crisis
Lewis W. Moncrief

One hundred years ago at almost any location in the United States, potable water was no farther away than the closest brook or stream. Today there are hardly any streams in the United States, except in a few high mountainous reaches, that can safely satisfy human thirst without chemical treatment. An oft-mentioned satisfaction in the lives of urbanites in an earlier era was a leisurely stroll in late afternoon to get a breath of fresh air in a neighborhood park or along a quiet street. Today in many of our major metropolitan areas it is difficult to find a quiet, peaceful place to take a leisurely stroll and sometimes impossible to get a breath of fresh air. These contrasts point up the dramatic changes that have occurred in the quality of our environment.

It is not my intent in this article, however, to document the existence of an environmental crisis but rather to discuss the cultural basis for such a crisis. Particular attention will be given to the institutional structures as expressions of our culture.

SOCIAL ORGANIZATION

In her book entitled *Social Institutions (1)*, J. O. Hertzler classified all social institutions into nine functional categories: (i) economic and industrial, (ii) matrimonial and domestic, (iii) political, (iv) religious, (v) ethical, (vi) educational, (vii) communications, (viii) esthetic, and (ix) health. Institutions exist to carry on each of these functions in all cultures, regardless of their location or relative complexity. Thus, it is not surprising that one of the analytical criteria used by anthropologists in the study of various cultures is the comparison and contrast of the various social institutions as to form and relative importance (2).

A number of attempts have been made to explain attitudes and behavior that are commonly associated with one institutional function as the result of influence from a presumably independent institutional factor. The classic example of such an analysis is *The Protestant Ethic and the Spirit of Capitalism* by Max Weber (3). In this significant work Weber attributes much of the economic and industrial growth in Western Europe and North America to capitalism, which, he argued, was an economic form that developed as a result of the religious teachings of Calvin, particularly spiritual determinism.

Social scientists have been particularly active in attempting to assess the influence of religious teaching and practice and of economic motivation on other institutional forms and behavior and on each other. In this connection, L. White (4) suggested that the exploitative attitude that has prompted much of the environmental crisis in Western Europe and North America is a result of the teachings of the Judeo-Christian tradition, which conceives of man as superior to all other creation and of everything else as created for his use and enjoyment. He goes on to contend that the only way to reduce the ecologic crisis which we are now facing is to "reject the Christian axiom that nature has no reason for existence save to serve man." As with other ideas that appear to be new and novel, Professor White's observations have begun to be widely circulated and accepted in scholarly circles, as witness the article by religious writer E. B. Fiske in the *New York Times* earlier this year (5). In this article, note is taken of the fact that several prominent theologians and theological groups have accepted this basic premise that Judeo-Christian doctrine regarding man's relation to the rest of creation is at the root of the West's environmental crisis. I would suggest that the wide acceptance of such a simplistic explanation is at this point based more on fad than on fact.

Certainly, no fault can be found with White's statement that "Human ecology is deeply conditioned by beliefs about our nature and destiny—that is, by religion." However, to argue that it is the primary conditioner of human behavior toward the environment is much more than the data that he cites to support this proposition will bear. For example, White himself notes very early in his article that there is evidence for the idea that man has been dramatically altering his environment since antiquity. If this be true, and there is evidence that it is, then this mediates against the idea that the Judeo-Christian religion uniquely predisposes cultures within which it thrives to exploit their natural resources with indiscretion. White's own examples weaken his argument considerably. He points out that human intervention in the periodic flooding of the Nile River basin and the fire-drive method of hunting by prehistoric man have both probably wrought significant "unnatural" changes in man's environment. The absence of Judeo-Christian influence in these cases is obvious.

It seems tenable to affirm that the role played by religion in man-to-man and man-to-environment relationships is one of establishing a very broad system of allowable beliefs and behavior and of articulating and invoking a system of social and spiritual rewards for those who conform and of negative sanctions for individuals or groups who approach or cross the pale of the religiously unacceptable. In other words, it defines the ball park in which the game is played, and, by the very nature of the park, some types of games cannot be played. However, the kind of game that ultimately evolves is not itself defined by the ball park. For example, where animism is practiced, it is not likely that the believers will indiscriminately destroy objects of nature because such activity would incur the danger of spiritual and social sanctions. However, the fact that another culture does not associate spiritual beings with natural objects does not mean that such a culture will invariably ruthlessly exploit its resources. It simply means that there are fewer social and psychological constraints against such action.

In the remainder of this article, I present an alternative set of hypotheses based on cultural variables which, it seems to me, are more plausible and more defensible as an explanation of the environmental crisis that is now confronting us.

No culture has been able to completely screen out the egocentric tendencies of human beings. There also exists in all cultures a status hierarchy of positions and values, with certain groups partially or totally excluded from access to these normatively desirable goals. Historically, the differences in most cultures between the "rich" and the "poor" have been great. The many very poor have often produced the wealth for the few who controlled the means of production. There may have been no alternative where scarcity of supply and unsatiated demand were economic reality. Still, the desire for a "better life" is universal; that is, the desire for higher status positions and the achievement of culturally defined desirable goals is common to all societies.

THE EXPERIENCE IN THE WESTERN WORLD

In the West two significant revolutions that occurred in the eighteenth and nineteenth centuries completely redirected its political, social, and economic destiny (6). These two types of revolutions were unique to the West until very recently. The French revolution marked the beginnings of widespread democratization. In specific terms, this revolution involved a redistribution of the means of production and a reallocation of the natural and human resources that are an integral part of the production process. In effect new channels of social mobility were created, which theoretically made more wealth accessible to more people. Even though the revolution was partially perpetrated in the guise of overthrowing the control of presumably Christian institutions and of destroying the influence of God over the minds of men, still it would be superficial to argue that Christianity did not influence this revolution. After all, biblical teaching is one of the strongest of all pronouncements concerning human dignity and individual worth.

At about the same time but over a more extended period, another kind of revolution was taking place, primarily in England. As White points out very well, this phenomenon, which began with a number of technological innovations, eventually consummated a marriage with natural science and began to take on the character that it has retained until today *(7)*. With this revolution the productive capacity of each worker was amplified by several times his potential prior to the revolution. It also became feasible to produce goods that were not previously producible on a commercial scale.

Later, with the integration of the democratic and the technological ideals, the increased wealth began to be distributed more equitably among the population. In addition, as the capital to land ratio increased in the production process and the demand grew for labor to work in the factories, large populations from the agrarian hinterlands began to concentrate in the emerging industrial cities. The stage was set for the development of the conditions that now exist in the Western world.

With growing affluence for an increasingly large segment of the population, there generally develops an increased demand for goods and services. The usual by-product of this affluence is waste from both the production and consumption processes. The disposal of that waste is further complicated by the high concentration of heavy waste producers in urban areas. Under these conditions the maxim that "Dilution is the solution to pollution" does not withstand the test of time, because the volume of such wastes is greater than the system can absorb and purify through natural means. With increasing population, increasing production, increasing urban concentrations, and increasing real median incomes for well over a hundred years, it is not surprising that our environment has taken a terrible beating in absorbing our filth and refuse.

THE AMERICAN SITUATION

The North American colonies of England and France were quick to pick up the technical and social innovations that were taking place in their motherlands. Thus, it is not surprising that the inclination to develop an industrial and manufacturing base is observable rather early in the colonies. A strong trend toward democratization also evidenced itself very early in the struggle for nationhood. In fact, Thistlewaite notes the significance of the concept of democracy as embodied in French thought to the framers of constitutional government in the colonies (8, pp. 33-34, 60).

From the time of the dissolution of the Roman Empire, resource ownership in the Western world was vested primarily with the monarchy or the Roman Catholic Church, which in turn bestowed control of the land resources on vassals who pledged fealty to the sovereign. Very slowly the concept of private ownership developed during the Middle Ages in Europe, until it finally developed into the fee simple concept.

In America, however, national policy from the outset was designed to convey ownership of the land and other natural resources into the hands of the citizenry. Thomas Jefferson was perhaps more influential in crystallizing this philosophy in the new nation than anyone else. It was his conviction that an agrarian society made up of small landowners would furnish the most stable foundation for building the nation (8, pp. 59-68). This concept has received support up to the present and, against growing economic pressures in recent years, through government programs that have encouraged the conventional family farm. This point is clearly relevant to the subject of this article because it explains how the natural resources of the nation came to be controlled not by a few aristocrats but by many citizens. It explains how decisions that ultimately degrade the environment are made not only by corporation boards and city engineers but by millions of owners of our natural resources. This is democracy exemplified!

CHALLENGE OF THE FRONTIER

Perhaps the most significant interpretation of American history has been Fredrick Jackson Turner's much criticized thesis that the western frontier was the prime force in shaping our society *(9)*. In his own words,

> If one would understand why we are today one nation, rather than a collection of isolated states, he must study this economic and social consolidation of the country. . . . The effect of the Indian frontier as a consolidating agent in our history is important.

He further postulated that the nation experienced a series of frontier challenges that moved across the continent in waves. These included the explorers' and traders' frontier, the Indian frontier, the cattle frontier, and three distinct agrarian frontiers. His thesis can be extended to interpret the expansionist period of our history in Panama, in Cuba, and in the Philippines as a need for a continued frontier challenge.

Turner's insights furnish a starting point for suggesting a second variable in analyzing the cultural basis of the United States' environmental crisis. As the nation began to expand westward, the settlers faced many obstacles, including a primitive transportation system, hostile Indians, and the absence of physical and social security. To many frontiersmen, particularly small farmers, many of the natural resources that are now highly valued were originally perceived more as obstacles than as assets. Forests needed to be cleared to permit farming. Marshes needed to be drained. Rivers needed to be controlled. Wildlife often represented a competitive threat in addition to being a source of food. Sod was considered a nuisance—to be burned, plowed, or otherwise destroyed to permit "desirable" use of the land.

Undoubtedly, part of this attitude was the product of perceiving these resources as inexhaustible. After all, if a section of timber was put to the torch to clear it for farming, it made little difference because there was still plenty to be had very easily. It is no coincidence that the "First Conservation Movement" began to develop about 1890. At that point settlement of the frontier was almost complete. With the passing of the frontier era of American history, it began to dawn on people that our resources were indeed exhaustible. This realization ushered in a new philosophy of our national government toward natural resources management under the guidance of Theodore Roosevelt and Gifford Pinchot. Samuel Hays *(10)* has characterized this movement as the appearance of a new "Gospel of Efficiency" in the management and utilization of our natural resources.

THE PRESENT AMERICAN SCENE

America is the archetype of what happens when democracy, technology, urbanization, capitalistic mission, and antagonism (or apathy) toward natural environment are blended together. The present situation is characterized by three dominant features that mediate against quick solution to this impending crisis: (i) an absence of personal moral direction concerning our treatment of our natural resources, (ii) an inability on the part of our social institutions to make adjustments to this stress, and (iii) an abiding faith in technology.

The first characteristic is the absence of personal moral direction. There is moral disparity when a corporation executive can receive a prison sentence for embezzlement but be congratulated for increasing profits by ignoring pollution abatement laws. That the absolute cost to society of the second act may be infinitely greater than the first is often not even considered.

The moral principle that we are to treat others as we would want to be treated seems as appropriate a guide as it ever has been. The rarity of such teaching and the even more uncommon instance of its being practiced help to explain how one municipality can, without scruple, dump its effluent into a stream even though it may do irreparable damage to the resource and add tremendously to the cost incurred by downstream municipalities that use the same water. Such attitudes are not restricted to any one culture. There appears to be an almost universal tendency to maximize self-interests and a widespread willingness to shift production costs to society to promote individual ends.

Undoubtedly, much of this behavior is the result of ignorance. If our accounting systems were more efficient in computing the cost of such irresponsibility both to the present generation and to those who will inherit the environment we are creating, steps would undoubtedly be taken to enforce compliance with measures designed to conserve resources and protect the environment. And perhaps if the total costs were known, we might optimistically speculate that more voluntary compliance would result.

A second characteristic of our current situation involves institutional inadequacies. It has been said that "what belongs to everyone belongs to no one." This maxim seems particularly appropriate to the problem we are discussing. So much of our environment is so apparently abundant that it is considered a free commodity. Air and water are particularly good examples. Great liberties have been permitted in the use and abuse of these resources for at least two reasons. First, these resources have typically been considered of less economic value than other natural resources except when conditions of extreme scarcity impose limiting factors. Second, the right of use is more difficult to establish for resources that are not associated with a fixed location.

Government, as the institution representing the corporate interests of all its citizens, has responded to date with dozens of legislative acts and numerous court decisions which give it authority to regulate the use of natural resources. However, the decisiveness to act has thus far been generally lacking. This indecisiveness cannot be understood without noting that the simplistic models that depict the conflict as that of a few powerful special interests versus "The People" are altogether inadequate. A very large proportion of the total citizenry is implicated in environmental degradation; the responsibility ranges from that of the board and executives of a utility company who might wish to thermally pollute a river with impunity to that of the average citizen who votes against a bond issue to improve the efficiency of a municipal sanitation system in order to keep his taxes from being raised. The magnitude of irresponsibility among individuals and institutions might be characterized as falling along a continuum from highly irresponsible to indirectly responsible. With such a broad base of interests being threatened with every change in resource policy direction, it is not surprising, although regrettable, that government has been so indecisive.

A third characteristic of the present American scene is an abiding faith in technology. It is very evident that the idea that technology can overcome almost any problem is widespread in Western society. This optimism exists in the face of strong evidence that much of man's technology, when misused, has produced harmful results, particularly in the long run. The reasoning goes something like this: "After all, we have gone to the moon. All we need to do is allocate enough money and brainpower and we can solve any problem."

It is both interesting and alarming that many people view technology almost as something beyond human control. Rickover put it this way *(11)*:

It troubles me that we are so easily pressured by purveyors of technology into permitting so-called "progress" to alter our lives without attempting to control it—as if technology were an irrepressible force of nature to which we must meekly submit.

He goes on to add:

It is important to maintain a humanistic attitude toward technology; to recognize clearly that since it is the product of human effort, technology can have no legitimate purpose but to serve man—man in general, not merely some men; future generations, not merely those who currently wish to gain advantage for themselves; man in the totality of his humanity, encompassing all his manifold interests and needs, not merely some one particular concern of his. When viewed humanistically, technology is seen not as an end in itself but a means to an end, the end being determined by man himself in accordance with the laws prevailing in his society.

In short, it is one thing to appreciate the value of technology; it is something else entirely to view it as our environmental savior—which will save us in spite of ourselves.

CONCLUSION

The forces of democracy, technology, urbanization, increasing individual wealth, and an aggressive attitude toward nature seem to be directly related to the environmental crisis now being confronted in the Western world. The Judeo-Christian tradition has probably influenced the character of each of these forces. However, to isolate religious tradition as a cultural component and to contend that it is the "historical root of our ecological crisis" is a bold affirmation for which there is little historical or scientific support.

To assert that the primary cultural condition that has created our environmental crisis is Judeo-Christian teaching avoids several hard questions. For example: Is there less tendency for those who control the resources in non-Christian cultures to live in extravagant affluence with attendant high levels of waste and inefficient consumption? If non-Judeo-Christian cultures had the same levels of economic productivity, urbanization, and high average household incomes, is there evidence to indicate that these cultures would not exploit or disregard nature as our culture does?

If our environmental crisis is a "religious problem," why are other parts of the world experiencing in various degrees the same environmental problems that we are so well acquainted with in the Western world? It is readily observable that the science and technology that developed on a large scale first in the West have been adopted elsewhere. Judeo-Christian tradition has not been adopted as a predecessor to science and technology on a comparable scale. Thus, all White can defensibly argue is that the West developed modern science and technology *first*. This says nothing about the origin or existence of a particular ethic toward our environment.

In essence, White has proposed this simple model:

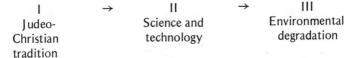

I	→	II	→	III
Judeo-Christian tradition		Science and technology		Environmental degradation

I have suggested here that, at best, Judeo-Christian teaching has had only an indirect effect on the treatment of our environment. The model could be characterized as follows:

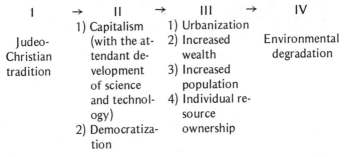

I	→	II	→	III	→	IV
Judeo-Christian tradition		1) Capitalism (with the attendant development of science and technology) 2) Democratization		1) Urbanization 2) Increased wealth 3) Increased population 4) Individual resource ownership		Environmental degradation

Even here, the link between Judeo-Christian tradition and the proposed dependent variables certainly has the least empirical support. One need only look at the veritable mountain of criticism of Weber's conclusions in *The Protestant Ethic and the Spirit of Capitalism* to sense the tenuous nature of this link. The second and third phases of this model are common to many parts of the world. Phase I is not.

Jean Mayer *(12)*, the eminent food scientist, gave an appropriate conclusion about the cultural basis for our environmental crisis:

> It might be bad in China with 700 million poor people but 700 million rich Chinese would wreck China in no time. . . . It's the rich who wreck the environment . . . occupy much more space, consume more of each natural resource, disturb ecology more, litter the landscape . . . and create more pollution.

REFERENCES AND NOTES

1. J. O. Hertzler, *Social Institutions* (McGraw-Hill, New York, 1929), pp. 47-64.
2. L. A. White, *The Science of Culture* (Farrar, Straus & Young, New York, 1949), pp. 121-145.
3. M. Weber, *The Protestant Ethic and the Spirit of Capitalism*, translated by T. Parsons (Scribner's, New York, 1958).
4. L.White, Jr., *Science* 155, 1203 (1967).
5. E. B. Fiske, "The link between faith and ecology," *New York Times* (4 January 1970), section 4, p. 5.
6. R. A. Nisbet, *The Sociological Tradition* (Basic Books, New York, 1966), pp. 21-44. Nisbet gives here a perceptive discourse on the social and political implications of the democratic and industrial revolutions to the Western world.
7. It should be noted that a slower and less dramatic process of democratization was evident in English history at a much earlier date than the French revolution. Thus, the concept of democracy was probably a much more pervasive influence in English than in French life. However, a rich body of philosophic literature regarding the rationale for democracy resulted from the French revolution. Its counterpart in English literature is much less conspicuous. It is an interesting aside to suggest that perhaps the industrial revolution would not have been possible except for the more broad-based ownership of the means of production that resulted from the long-standing process of democratization in England.
8. F. Thistlewaite, *The Great Experiment* (Cambridge Univ. Press, London, 1955).
9. F. J. Turner, *The Frontier in American History* (Henry Holt, New York, 1920 and 1947).
10. S. P. Hays, *Conservation and the Gospel of Efficiency* (Harvard Univ. Press, Cambridge, Mass., 1959).
11. H. G. Rickover, *Amer. Forests* 75, 13 (August 1969).
12. J. Mayer and T. G. Harris, *Psychol. Today* 3, 46 and 48 (January 1970).

I believe a leaf of grass is no less than the journey-work of the stars,
And the pismire is equally perfect, and a grain of sand, and the egg of
   the wren,
And the tree-toad is a chef-d'oeuvre for the highest,
And the running blackberry would adorn the parlors of heaven,
And the narrowest hinge in my hand puts to scorn all machinery,
And the cow crunching with depress'd head surpasses any statue,
And a mouse is miracle enough to stagger sextillions of infidels.

Walt Whitman

The Population
Explosion and the
Rights of the
Subhuman World

John B. Cobb, Jr.

Only a short time ago it seemed necessary to cry out with passion against the massive indifference and silence on the subject of the population explosion and the resulting ecological crisis. Today, almost miraculously, the cry has been heard, and these problems have moved to the center of the national debate. This does not mean that the task has been accomplished. Far from it. The ecologists and demographers still warn that unless aroused public opinion is quickly concretized in drastic political action it may prove too little and too late. Indeed, there are many indications that it is already too late to save much of the world from catastrophic famine sometime in the next decade.

The problem that we face has been long in the making and, if the most terrible of the possible outcomes is avoided, one that will remain with us for a long time. A major factor in bringing about the crisis and the long delay of its serious recognition has been Western man's fundamental perception of himself in relation to the subhuman world. Even now his basic vision inhibits the full acknowledgment of the crisis and deters him from needed actions. Unless our underlying self-understanding is changed, it will be difficult indeed to take the steps required for satisfactory human survival and to adopt the new mode of life that a new situation demands.

Few principles have been more deeply accepted as normative in the Western psyche than the absolute value of every human individual. Of course, the actions of nations and individuals have repeatedly violated the implications of this principle, but that is not the point here. The positive effect of the principle on national and individual action has been enormous. Vast efforts have been expended to keep alive human beings whether or not they were able to make a contribution to society. A large portion of scientific and technological advancement has been successfully directed toward the conquest of disease and the prolongation of life.

If it is objected that the increase of life expectancy and the accompanying population explosion are due to scientific and technological advance rather than to the prizing of individual life, the reply is that the rise of science and technology has itself been at least partly a function of the particular view of nature and man characteristic especially of Western European Christianity. Here, man has been separated from nature as its observer and master, and nature has been so desacralized as to leave it open for his uninhibited investigation and manipulation. The absolute value of the human has been associated with the view of nature as lacking all intrinsic value. The subhuman world has its value only as instrumental to human value.

Retrospectively it can then be said with some confidence that the absolute valuation of human individuals and the view of the subhuman world only as means to human ends have provided the attitudinal context within which the present crisis has developed. In itself this does not determine whether these convictions are true or false or whether they are adequate also as the context for responding to the crisis.

Let us consider the possibility of reaffirming our historic convictions. To what consequences might this lead? First, it might mean that we would continue basically on the course we have begun. We would then view the progressive breakdown of the ecological cycle as reason for accelerating our scientific investigations and technological progress. We have already moved far toward substituting an artificial environment for a natural one. If the planet cannot support both a vastly increased human population and high grades of subhuman life, we will give up the latter and learn to produce what we need artificially out of the inanimate resources of the planet or from the lowest grades of the animate. We would build vast cities under plastic domes surrounded by poisoned air, polluted water, rock and dust. The subhuman world would then indeed be little more than the mere "it" we have treated it as being.

No one today really knows whether such a direction is even possible. Could science and technology sustain a larger population in this wholly artificial context than can be sustained by achieving ecological balance? Would it turn out that man has either biological or psychological needs that could not be met in this way? Would the changes in temperature, sea level, radiation, and so forth be so drastic that survival would be impossible despite every technological advance?

Even if it were possible, one may question the wisdom of those who would choose it. Although the attempt to evaluate a type of life profoundly different from any we have known is fraught with hazards, it is difficult to think of existence in such a world as even human, much less happy. The absolutization of human life at the total expense of subhuman life seems to lead to a mode of being in which human existence itself would be subhuman in quality.

In any case, we know that we do not presently have the science or technology to sustain human life on a dead planet. If we press on in this direction, most of the world's present population and its immediate offspring must be sacrificed. Perhaps a hundred or a thousand years from now men will be faced with a serious choice between increasing population and retaining a living environment, but today the living context remains essential to the maintenance of human life as well.

On this ground alone, then, one who retains the traditional evaluation of man and nature should agree to devote our vast energies to nursing the environment back to health while stabilizing population. At present, subhuman life is necessary to man's existence and hence, of immeasurable instrumental value. The question of its ultimate dispensability is academic.

Certainly in our present emergency those who absolutize the gulf between man and other living things have every reason to share in the effort to save the environment for at least the immediate future. Still, one must question the adequacy of this approach even for the decisions that lie near at hand. Can those who are indifferent to the preservation of subhuman life except as it is instrumental to human life develop the patience and restraint that are now needed? Let us suppose that wilderness plays a crucial role in the ecological balance of the planet. Will one who is interested in wilderness *only* because of its very indirect importance to sustaining and enriching human life, oppose with sufficient firmness the strong economic and humanistic arguments for converting it to more direct uses? Or will those whose only interest in the ocean is as a resource for human ends struggle with sufficient vigor against its use as the final repository for waste—a use which in the short run may assist in reducing the pollution of men's more immediate environment?

These questions are analogous to those that must be directed toward any theory of enlightened self-interest as an adequate guide to conduct. If a nation really cares little for the good of any people besides its own, does the fact that in the very long run its own people will benefit most from worldwide peace and prosperity restrain it from seizing opportunities for short run gains at the expense of others? The overwhelming evidence is that it does not. The pure rationality of very long-term self-interest is powerless against the passion for immediate advantage. It is almost inconceivable that the American people will make *major* economic sacrifices and drastically alter their way of life *only* for the sake of a later and a larger good. Each particular sacrifice and individual alteration seems trivial, and the consequences are in any case too remote and uncertain to motivate.

Let me hasten to say that although enlightened self-interest is insufficient alone, it is at least equally true to say that nothing can happen without it. Although I believe that the more enlightened aspects of American foreign policy since World War II would not have been operative apart from a widespread humanistic idealism, none of them would have become operative if long-term advantages to the United States had not also been visible. Although emphasis will be upon the vision that shapes ideals, I hope I will not be understood as supposing that ideals can have much social efficacy when their pursuit is not sustained by self-interest.

My argument thus far has been that the inherited vision of an absolute gulf in value between men as ends and the rest of the world as means is logically but not actually sufficient to motivate the actions now needed. Man will, in fact, care for the subhuman world sufficiently to heal it and to adjust himself to its needs only if he views it has having some claim upon him, some intrinsic right to exist and to prosper.

If our own dominant tradition is not adequate to provide the context for the actions we must now perform, where can we turn? One possibility that immediately occurs to many is a return to a primitive feeling for man's participation in the whole of nature and his sense of its sacredness.

In *The Making of a Counter Culture*, Theodore Roszak quotes a Wintu Indian woman describing the contrasting relationship of her shamanistic culture and that of the white man to a common environment.

> The white people never cared for the land or deer or bear. When we Indians kill meat, we eat it all up. When we dig roots, we make little holes. . . . We shake down acorns and pinenuts. We don't chop down the trees. We only use dead wood. But the white people plow up the ground, pull up the trees, kill everything. The tree says, 'Don't. I am sore. Don't hurt me.' But they chop it down and cut it up. The spirit of the land hates them. . . . The Indians never hurt anything, but the white people destroy all. They blast rocks and scatter them on the ground. The rock says, 'Don't! You are hurting me.' But the white people pay no attention. When the Indians use rocks, they take little round ones for

their cooking. . . . How can the spirit of the earth like the white
man? . . . Everywhere the white man has touched it, it is
sore.

In hearing such a passage we can immediately sense its
ecological significance. Here is a people who seek in every way
they can to interfere as little as possible with their environment. Their motivation is not the anthropocentric one we
have been considering, but rather a concern for trees and
rocks that is like the concern for other human beings. Of
course, self-interest plays a role, since they desire that the
spirit of the earth like them. Clearly, what dominates is not a
pragmatic estimate of consequences to themselves. They have
observed the white man getting away with it for generations.

Is this primitive view the one that is needed? Despite its
attractiveness, surely the answer is negative. If men had
remained at this primitive level, it is true, the ecological crisis
would not have arisen. The human population of the planet
would have remained small. Pollution would have been
minimal. Measured by *these* standards, we might judge that
the history that separates us from the primitive is a long story
of a fall.

However, there are other standards as well. Primitive life
has many drawbacks, to put it mildly. Perhaps it was not
always nasty, brutish, and short, but certainly for the individual it was much more precarious than ours, even if the threat
of total human extinction was less. Although the concern for
nature appears admirable, we must remember to what extent
it was motivated by irrational fear. Often trees and rocks
were felt as more sacred than the lives of members of another
tribe or even perhaps of one's own. There is both nobility and
savagery in primitive life as there is in the lives of people at
every level of civilization.

If we were so foolish as to attempt to return to a primitive
world, the vast majority of us would have to die. Our depleted environment in the United States could not support

even the equivalent of the Indian population found by Europeans on their arrival, if we sought to live as they did, and that was a very small population in comparison with ours. In the process of change, much of what we most prize in human existence would be lost for even the few survivors. If the choice were between moving forward toward a wholly artificial environment in which technology almost wholly replaced nature and returning to a primitive existence, we would be forced to choose the former, however horrible it might be. There is never any possibility of return to the past, however idyllic that may appear, and if we could and did return, we would be appalled by the actuality of what we found.

Is there another possibility before us besides these two dreary alternatives of producing an artificial environment or returning to a primitive state? I believe that there is, and that it can be found by altering our view in a way that is continuous with a line of development we have followed rather than by reversing the basic course of our history. As different as this is from projecting our present stance into the future, it is even more different from returning to some past position.

Israel drew itself out of the primitive immersion in nature by affirming man's primacy within nature. Her vision of God's transcendence desacralized nature. The existence of the Wintu Indians' "spirit of the earth" was denied. Nature was given to man for his well-being.

Nevertheless, nature was not reduced simply to means. In that first chapter of Genesis, so fateful for the course of human events, God declares again and again that the subhuman world is good. He declares this quite without reference to man. Its goodness is intrinsic. It shares with man the status of creaturehood. It participates with him in witnessing to God's greatness. Thus man is freed to govern the world, but the world that he governs is not thereby reduced to mere means to his end.

In *The Structure of Christian Existence,* I argue that Christianity introduces a more radical self-transcendence. The intensification of freedom and individuality that is involved separates man from the subhuman environment even more drastically than did the personal existence of the Jew. At the same time the contrast between what is and what ought to be, already vividly developed in Jewish apocalypticism, is intensified. Original sin and its cosmic consequences are keenly felt. Man is turned toward God and his fellow man, and his natural environment almost loses significance. What emerges is an extreme humanism, a strong sense of man's deep internality, his infinitely important selfhood, and his radical transcendence over the subhuman world. The profoundly self-conscious individual could be saved from the misery of self-preoccupation only by authentic love of others.

I argue that not only is love essential to the Christian in a new way but that the quality of his love is new. Whereas love of the neighbor for the Jew meant justice and righteousness in the treatment of the neighbor, love of the neighbor for the Christian means an actual concern for him in his recognized otherness. Obviously such concern should express itself in just and righteous treatment, but it is not motivated by the desire to be righteous. In that sense it is the motiveless motive of Christian action. It is directly connected with the absolute valuation of every individual life, which we have recognized as the foundation of our traditional ideals.

It is my present contention that this high valuation of human life in its individuality and particularity is susceptible to two developments in relation to the subhuman world. On the one hand, focusing upon what is distinctively human and inward tends to widen the gulf between man and other living things. This can lead, and has indeed led, to the absolutization of this gulf that has dominated modern Western ideals. The second possible development is that the concern for the other in his otherness that is directed toward the fellow human being can be extended to subhuman life as well. This extension of love has been a subdominant element in modern Western idealism, gaining clear expression in St. Francis and

Albert Schweitzer, in some of the romantics, such as Wordsworth, and in some naturalists, such as Loren Eiseley. Here there is a disinterested love of nature quite unlike the primitive sacralization, transcending the Old Testament recognition of the goodness of all creation. This love of nature involves no disparagement of man, for he is the apex and summation of nature. It need not prevent man from continuing his scientific investigations of nature. Indeed, it can provide such inquiry with a deeper motivation, a level of motivation that has been lacking since the acids of modernity destroyed the vision of divinely imposed order so important to the great scientists of the seventeenth century. It need not altogether reject technological manipulation of nature where that is needed for the sake of a richer life for man, but it would prevent ruthless indifference to the consequences of our actions for the living environment. Every human action must be measured in terms of its consequences both for man and for other living things. That man is of vastly greater worth than any other creature does not reduce the value of the other to nothing.

I am persuaded that some such perception of ourselves and our world, a perception that is an extension of the Christian love of the neighbor, would provide us with the context we need. It is already present in one current of the Western tradition. It has expressed itself in the uniquely Western and significantly named "humane society." It seems to have considerable appeal both to the common sense of those "over thirty" and to the contemporary youth culture. All that we know about evolution supports this vision. Why then can it not be readily and immediately adopted?

The chief question, it seems, is that of truth. Are subhuman entities fit objects of love, or is it only as we project being and meaning upon them that they can be loved? If the latter, then the love is indeed sentimentality. One cannot continue to be concerned about something in its otherness, while believing that it has no real value or existence in that otherness. Furthermore, the modern Western philosophic tradition, by and large, leads to this negative conclusion. This tradition has been deeply shaped by its Christian background; but it is important for our present purposes that it is this tradition, and not the Biblical vision as such, that has caused the dominant culture to dismiss the claims of the romantic perception of nature to provide insight into its reality. That distinction leaves open the possibility of a different response to the environment that is yet authentically Christian.

The title of this article is "The Population Explosion and the Rights of the Subhuman World." Little has been said of the former. It is, of course, the occasion of our concern for the latter, since if it continues unchecked there is virtually no chance of preserving nonhuman life on any significant scale. Whether we should check it is thus in part a function of our judgment of the seriousness of the loss that would be involved in the destruction of most nonhuman life on the planet. I have been suggesting that this loss would be very serious indeed even if human life could continue indefinitely without the matrix that has thus far sustained it. The ideal that follows appropriately from my vision of the place of man in nature is that of the planet having the maximum human population that can attain a rich and meaningful life in stable interaction with as great a variety of other forms of life as possible. What that population would be I do not know. Some argue that it could only be a billion or so. Others may reasonably claim that with the advance of technology the human population could expand greatly beyond its present size without destroying its environment. These are factual questions to be worked out in time. At present, it is quite clear that population growth is not occurring without the most serious consequences to the environment and that the presently available technology cannot solve the world's problems unless the rate of growth is greatly reduced and perhaps even reversed.

Just as important as control of population is control of the unnecessary consumption of resources by the prosperous portion of mankind, which means by us. There must be a shaping of new images of the rich life in which richness is not measured by economic standards. Individually and collectively we should rapidly consider how to simplify our lives and immediately resist the pressure of advertising and of peer practice to indulge in new luxuries which we know in a short time come to seem like necessities. We need to develop a new asceticism based not on economics but on ecology.

In the foregoing, I have said almost nothing about God. That is intentional. If survival is dependent on a widespread vivification of belief in God, we are indeed in trouble. To alter our sense of the reality and value of our natural environment will be difficult enough, but there we have at least some cultural trends on our side. At the moment we should use our theological perspective on the present situation to call for an enhanced concern for the subhuman world for its own sake as well as for our own and to undergird the growth of such concern with a cognitive account of the world and man's place in it. That is a contribution that a secularized culture may be able to understand and appreciate. Today theology needs to be a part of that culture.

However, theology has its own more specialized task as well and that task centers around God and belief in him. In speaking to myself as theologian and to whomever else will hear, this concern remains crucial for me. We may (and must) operate much of the time at the penultimate level and even as if the penultimate level were ultimate. But it is not. There is value to both man and nature, but viewed in themselves, simply as they are, this value is ephemeral indeed. In cold detachment one cannot help wondering whether it really matters very much if this endless series of little values continues. Perhaps a lifeless planet in which suffering as well as joy had come once and for all to an end is not after all so much to be avoided. Is it not possible that our Western post-

Christian insistence that life is good is now an ungrounded remnant of a once vigorous belief in God? Can it survive indefinitely apart from that belief? And if it does not survive is there another basis on which men can successfully be called to sacrifice their present happiness for the survival of their species? At least here there is cause for concern.

Similarly, the projection of trends at the penultimate level is profoundly depressing. Those who seek to galvanize us into action by describing the likely disastrous consequences of our treatment of our environment are always in danger of undercutting the motivation to the action for which they call. Indeed, the information they give us combined with our general knowledge of human nature is grounds for despair rather than action and not a few have already recognized this and responded accordingly.

How can the logic of despair be avoided? Is it enough that our culture remains a fundamentally optimistic and activistic one? Can we simply assume that this heritage will carry us through? Should we recognize that this fundamental optimism roots also in belief in God? Can it be sustained at the level of the penultimate? Is the biologically grounded desire to live sufficient? What are we to make of cultures that teach resignation and release as the response to evil? Perhaps our need for vital faith in God is more pressing than is widely recognized.

Where faith exists, the recognition of the value of our natural environment in itself can be enriched and undergirded by belief in its value for God. I do not believe the latter can be substituted for the former. Unless the subhuman world has some value in itself, I do not see that it can or should have value to God. However, if it does have value in itself, and if that value is valuable also to God, then what is penultimate becomes also ultimate, what is ephemeral becomes everlasting, and what could be written off as unimportant is grounded beyond threat of denial.

Even if belief in God would help us, here, too, the question of truth arises. Most minds shaped by the dominant modern philosophy find no place for God. That this belief still lingers on is witness to some dimension of experience or human need poorly understood in that philosophy. That rationality and advanced education in our society tend to militate against belief in God is witness to the power of philosophic orthodoxy and to the direction in which it cuts on this matter.

I suggest that what has eroded belief in God is not unconnected with what has inhibited belief in the reality and value of the natural environment. If sense experience is primary, and God cannot be sensuously experienced, then at best he must be an inference. However, inference depends on real causal relations, and a philosophy built on sense experience has difficulty in comprehending real causal relations. Hence God is at best a postulate, and the status of postulates is obscure. Certainly they are remote from vivid religious experience and faith. Perhaps by concentrating on our reorientation to nature we will incidentally recover a context for speaking once again with conviction and plausibility about God. And perhaps that in turn will provide the secure ground we need for concern for nature on the one hand and hope on the other.

The newly discovered relationship of man as a partner in the adventure of all living things underlies much of the new ecological science and helps to account for the almost sudden concern of man for his environment and the effects of his actions upon it. Such concern was not possible to a mind that believed it held divinely given 'dominion' over the earth, nor to a mind that believed it operated outside the universal system altogether.

Kaiser News

Our Treatment of
the Environment in
Ideal and Actuality

Yi-Fu Tuan

Ethnocentrism is characteristic of peoples all over the world. It is difficult for any viable culture to avoid seeing itself as the center of light shading into darkness. In Europe, to be sure, in the late seventeenth and early eighteenth centuries, this glorification of self was temporarily reversed. *Là-bas on était bien*. In the spirit of that age Europe was viewed as a portion of the earth afflicted with the blight of tyranny and superstition; beyond lay unspoiled Nature, unspoiled and rational peoples still appareled in celestial light (1). This romantic spirit has continued to affect the thinking of the West to the present day. Sensitive Westerners are wont to contrast their own aggressive, exploitative attitude to nature with the harmonious relationships of other times and other places. This view should be commended for generosity, but it lacks realism and fails to recognize inconsistency and paradox as characteristic of human existence.

In recent years two ideas that have bearing on our relationships to our environment are receiving greater recognition. One is that the balances of nature can be upset by people with the most primitive tools, the other that a wide gap may exist between a culture's ideals and their expression in the real world.

A current debate of interest in connection with the first point is the role of man in the extinction of Pleistocene mammals. Although the issue is far from resolution, I think we must admit that Paul Martin has made a good case for what he calls "prehistoric overkill" *(2)*. We are readily persuaded that the disappearance of the bison was brought about by masterful and predatory white men, but find the thought that primitive hunters could cause the wholesale destruction of fauna somewhat unpalatable.

The second point is a commonplace of experience in daily life; that a highminded philosopher should actually live his philosophy is a matter for surprise, and we take it for granted that few of a politician's professed ideals are convertible into substance. But in the study of the ideas and ideals of cultures, especially non-Western cultures, there remains a tendency to assume that they have force and correspond to reality. It seems to go against the grain for a scientist to seek for polarities, dichotomies, and paradoxes; he would rather see unity and harmony. Contrarieties exist, however, in cultures as in individuals. A nonliterate, stable people such as the Zunis of New Mexico do indeed make much of their aspiration to achieve harmonious order in the affairs of nature and of men, but their community is nonetheless wrecked from time to time by bitter factionalism *(3)*.

If small and stable societies do not often work as harmonious wholes, it is not surprising that large and complex civilizations like those of Europe and China should contain numerous dysfunctions. One of these is ecological imbalance. This is a theme I wish to take up—but indirectly; my primary concern is with the gaps that exist between an expressed attitude toward environment and actual practice. Such gaps may be taken as one of the signs of maladjustment in society.

To the question, what is the basic difference between European and Chinese attitudes to nature, many people might answer that whereas the European sees nature as subordinate to man the Chinese sees himself as part of nature. Although there is some truth in this generalization, it cannot be pressed too far. A culture's publicized ethos about its environment seldom covers more than a fraction of the total range of its attitudes and practices pertaining to that environment. In the play of forces that govern the world, esthetic and religious ideals rarely have a major role.

Christianity has often been blamed for Western man's presumption of power over nature. Professor Lynn White *(4)*, for example, speaks of the Christian religion as the most anthropocentric the world has seen: it not only established a dualism between man and nature but insisted that it is God's will that man should exploit nature for proper ends. Christianity, White says, has destroyed antiquity's feeling for the sacredness of places and of natural things, and has made it possible for man to exploit his environment indifferent to the spirits that once guarded the trees, hills, and brooks. The Christian religion he further credits with Western man's prideful faith in perpetual progress, an idea that was unknown to Greco-Roman antiquity and to the Orient.

Opinions such as these reenforce the view that Christianity constituted a great divide. But the official triumph of Christ over the pagan deities brought no revolutionary change to the organization either of society or of nature. At the level of the actual impress of man on environment, both constructive and destructive, the pagan world had as much to show as Christianized Europe did, until the beginning of the modern period. Contrary to the commonly accepted opinion of twentieth-century scholars, classical antiquity knew progressivism. As Ludwig Edelstein has recently noted, the pre-Socratic philosopher Xenophanes believed in progress; and his faith could well have been buoyed up by the engineering achievements of this time *(5)*. Lines in Sophocles' *Antigone* refer to the power of man to tear the soil with his plow. Plato in *Critias* described the negative side of that power—deforestation and soil erosion *(6)*. By the early Hellenistic period, technical ingenuity was performing feats that justified Aristotle's boast: "Vanquished by nature, we become masters by technique" *(7)*.

But the Romans did far more than the Greeks to impose their will on the natural environment. "Public roads," as Gibbons wrote in admiration, "ran in a direct line from one city to another, with very little respect for the obstacles either of nature or of private property. Mountains were perforated, and bold arches thrown over the broadest and most rapid streams" (8). An even more overriding example of the triumph of the human will over the lineaments of nature is the Roman grid method of dividing up the land into *centuria quadrata*, each containing a hundred *heredia*. As John Bradford puts it (9), centuriation well displayed the arbitrary but methodical qualities in Roman government. With absolute self-assurance and great technical competence the Romans imposed the same formal pattern of land division on the well-watered alluvium of the Po Valley as on the near-desert of Tunisia. Even today the forceful imprint of centuriation can be traced across thousands of square miles on both sides of the central Mediterranean, and it can still stir the imagination by its scale and boldness.

Against this background of the vast transformations of nature in the pagan world, the inroads made in the early centuries of the Christian era appear relatively modest. Christianity teaches that man has dominion over nature—but for a long time this new dignity was more a tenet of faith than a fact of experience: for man's undisputed power over nature to become a realized fact Europe had to await the growth of human numbers, the achievement of greater administrative centralization, and the development and application of new technological skills. Farmsteads and arable fields multiplied at the expense of forests and marshes through the Middle Ages, but these lacked the permanence, the geometric order, and the prideful assertion of the human will that one can more readily read into the Roman road systems, aqueducts, and centuriated landholdings.

When we turn to China, we again find discrepancies between esthetic ideals and performance, as well as unforeseen conflicts and dysfunctions that are inevitable in a complex civilization. Western intellectuals who look at Chinese culture tend to be overgenerous, following the example of the eighteenth-century *philosophes* rather than the chauvinism of nineteenth-century European scholars.

Seduced by China's Taoist and Buddhist traditions, they like to compare the Oriental's quiescent and adaptive approach toward nature with the aggressive masculinity of Western man.

An adaptive attitude toward nature does indeed have ancient roots in China. Evidence of it occurs in diverse sources. Well-known to the West is the concept of *feng-shui* or geomancy, aptly defined as "the art of adapting the residences of the living and the dead so as to co-operate and harmonize with the local currents of the cosmic breath" *(10)*. A general effect of the belief in feng-shui has been to encourage a preference for natural curves—for winding paths and structures that seem to fit into the landscape rather than to dominate it—and at the same time to promote a distaste for straight lines and layouts.

Ancient Chinese literature contains scattered evidence that the need to regulate the use of resources was recognized. Even as early as the Eastern Chou period (8th—3rd century B.C.) the deforestation resulting from the expansion of agriculture and the building of cities seems to have led to an appreciation of the value of trees. In the *Chou Li*—a work which was probably compiled in the third century B.C. but may well include earlier material—two classes of conservation officials are mentioned: the inspectors of mountains and of forests. They were charged with protecting certain species, and with seeing to it that the common people cut trees at the proper season, except when emergencies required making coffins or strengthening dykes *(11)*. Another ancient literary reference to conservation practice is Mencius' advice to King Huai of Liang that he would not lack for wood if he allowed the people to cut trees only at the proper time *(12)*.

Throughout Chinese history perspicacious officials have on various occasions warned against the dire consequences of deforestation. They deplored the indiscriminate cutting of trees in the mountains not only because of its harmful effect on stream flow and on the quality of soil in the lowland but also because they believed that forested mountain ridges slowed down the horse-riding barbarians. As one scholar of the Ming dynasty put it, "I saw the fact that what the country relies on as strategically important is the mountain, and what the mountain relies on as a screen to prevent advance are the trees" (13). The scholar-officials also recognized the esthetic value of forested mountains. The Wu-tai mountains in northern Shan-hsi, for example, were famous, but shorn of their trees can they retain their fame?

These references suggest that an old tradition of forest care existed in China. On the other hand it is clear that the concern arose in response to damages that had already occurred, even in antiquity. Animistic belief and Taoist nature philosophy lie at the back of an adaptive attitude to environment; alone these might have produced a sequestered utopia. But China, with her gardens and temple compounds, was also a vast bureaucracy, a civilization, and an empire. Opposed to the attitude of passivity was the "male" principle of dominance. One of the greatest culture heroes of China was the semi-legendary Yu, whose fame lay not in his precepts but in his acts—his feats of engineering.

An idea that lent support to the dominance side in Chinese culture was one which discerned a model of the cosmos in the earthly environment. It held that the regular motions of the stars could be expressed architecturally and ritually in space and time on earth. The walled city was given a rectilinear pattern, an orientation, and a grandeur that reflected the order and dimension of heaven (14). The earth's surface itself lacks paradigms of geometric order. Mountains and water are irregularly disposed. Experience of them has led to such unaggressive precepts as the need to observe and placate the spirits of the earth, the need for man to contemplate terrestrial harmony and adapt himself to it. By contrast, observation of the stars has encouraged the aggressive side of Chinese culture, nurturing its predilections for order, hierarchy, and control.

Visitors to China in the nineteenth and early part of the twentieth centuries have often commented on the treelessness of the North, and the acute problems of soil erosion on the loess-covered plateaus. These areas were once well wooded. Deforestation on a vast scale took place as population increased and more and more land was taken over by farmers. But this alone does not account for the extent of the clearing. Other factors militated against prudence. One was the ancient custom, first recorded in the fourth century B.C., of burning trees in order to deprive dangerous animals of their hiding places *(15)*. Even in contemporary China farmers are known to start fires for no evident purpose.

Asked why, they may say it is to clear land for cultivation—although the extent of burning far exceeds the needs for this purpose—or it is to leave fewer places in which bandits may hide, or to encourage the growth of small-sized sprouts in the burnt-over area and avoid the labor of splitting wood *(16)*. The real reason for the burning is difficult to pin down.

Forests in North China were also depleted to make charcoal for industrial fuel. From the tenth century on, the expanding metallic industries swallowed up many hundred of thousands of tons of charcoal each year, as did the manufacture of salt, alum, bricks, tiles, and liquor. By the Sung dynasty (960—1279 A.D.) the demand for wood and charcoal as both household and industrial fuels had exceeded the timber resources of the country; the result was the increasing substitution of coal for wood and charcoal *(17)*.

An enormous amount of timber was needed for construction in the old Chinese cities, probably more than was required in European cities of comparable size. One reason for this is the dependence of traditional Chinese architecture on wood as the basic structural material. Great cities like Ch'ang-an, Lo-yang, and Hang-chou made severe demands on the resources of the surrounding country. The rapid expansion of Hang-chou in the thirteenth century to a metropolis of some one and a half million people led to the denuding of the neighboring hills. Despite the demand of the swelling urban population for food, some farmers found it more profitable to give up rice cultivation and grow trees *(18)*. Rebuilding the wooden houses after fires put a further strain on timber resources; but of greater consequence was the deliberate devastation of whole cities in times of upheaval, when rebels or nomadic invaders toppled a dynasty. The succeeding phase of reconstruction was normally achieved in haste by armies of men who made ruthless inroads on the forest.

In a complex society benign institutions can introduce effects that were no part of their original purpose. The indirect results of any major action or event are largely unpredictable, and we tend to see the irony only in retrospect. For example, Buddhism in China is at least partly responsible for the preservation of trees around temple compounds, islands of green in an otherwise denuded landscape. On the other hand Buddhism introduced into China the idea of cremation of the dead; and from the tenth to the fourteenth centuries cremation was common enough in the southeastern coastal provinces to create a timber shortage there *(19)*. Large parts of Mongolia have been overgrazed by sheep and goats. The most abused land appeared as sterile rings around the lamaseries, whose princely domains pastured large herds though the monks were not supposed to consume meat. In Japan, the seventeenth-century official and conservationist Kumazawa Banzan was inclined to put most of the blame for the deforestation of his country on Buddhism; the Buddhists, he contended, were responsible for seven-tenths of the nation's timber consumption. One reason for this grossly disproportionate consumption was that instead of living in "grass hermitages" they built themselves huge halls and temples *(20).*

Another example of fine irony concerns that most civilized of the arts: writing. Soot was needed to make black ink, and soot came from burnt pine. As E. H. Schafer has put it, "Even before T'ang times, the ancient pines of the mountains of Shang-tung had been reduced to carbon, and now the busy brushes of the vast T'ang bureaucracy were rapidly bringing baldness to the T'a-hang Mountains between Shansi and Hopei" *(21).*

Although ancient pines may already have disappeared from Shan-tung by the T'ang dynasty, from the testimony of the Japanese monk Ennin we know that large parts of the peninsula were still well wooded in the ninth century *(22).* The landscapes described by Ennin provide sharp contrast to the dry, bare scenes that characterize so much of Shan-tung in modern times. Shan-tung has many holy places; the province includes the sacred mountain T'ai-shan and the ancient state of Lu, which was the birthplace of Confucius. The numerous shrines and temples have managed to preserve only tiny spots of green amid the brown. Around Chiao-chou Bay in eastern Shan-tung a conspicuous strip of forest lies behind the port of Ch'ing-tao. It is ironic that this patch of green should owe its existence not to native piety but to the conservation-minded Germans.

The unplanned and often careless use of land in China belongs, one hopes, to the past. The Communist government has made an immense effort to control erosion and to reforest. Besides such large projects as shelterbelts along the semiarid edges of the North, forest brigades of the individual communes have planted billions of trees around villages, in cities, along roads and river banks, and on the hillsides. A visitor from New Zealand reported in 1960 that as seen from the air the new growths spread "a mist of green" over the once bare hills of South China *(23).* For those who admire the old culture, it must again seem ironic that the "mist of green" is no reflection of the traditional virtues of Taoism and Buddhism; on the contrary, it rests on their explicit denial *(24)*.

Problems of despoliation of the environment must be attacked along several fronts. Engineers offer technical solutions. Social scientists need to examine those societal dysfunctions that leave strains and scars on our habitats. One symptom of maladjustment lies in the conflicts between an ideal of Nature or environment and our practice. Such conflicts are embarrassing to observe for they expose our intellectual failure to make the connection, and perhaps also our hypocrisy; moreover, they cannot always be resolved. Contradictions of a certain kind may be inherent in the human condition, and not even stable and simple cultures are exempt. Ideals and necessities are frequently opposed as, for example, on the most fundamental level, keeping one's cake and eating it are incompatible. Some consume beauty for gain; but all of us must consume it to live.

REFERENCES

1. Willey, B. 1962. *The eighteenth-century background* (Penguin Books), pp. 19-21.
2. Martin, P. S. 1963. *The last 10,000 years* (Tucson: Univ. of Arizona Press), pp. 64-65, 70; P. S. Martin and H. E. Wright, Jr., eds., *Pleistocene extinctions*, Proc. of the 7th Congress of the Internat. Assoc. for Quaternary Research, vol. 6, New Haven: Yale Univ. Press, 1967.
3. Vogt, E., and E. M. Albert, eds. 1966. *People of Rimrock: A study of value in five cultures* (Cambridge: Harvard Univ. Press), pp. 201-2.
4. White, L. 1967. The historical roots of our ecologic crisis, *Science* 155:1205.
5. Edelstein, L. 1967. *The idea of progress in classical antiquity* (Baltimore, Md.: The Johns Hopkins Press), pp. 3, 11-13.
6. Sophocles, *Antigone*, trans. by Gilbert Murray, quoted in Arnold Toynbee, *Greek historical thought* (New York: New American Library, 1952), p. 128; Plato, *Critias*, ibid., pp. 146-47. On the theme of man-nature relationships in Western thought, see Clarence Glacken's monumental *Traces on the Rhodian shore*, Berkeley, Cal.: Univ. of California Press, 1967.
7. Aristotle, *Mechanics* 847, a 20.
8. Gibbons, E. *The decline and fall of the Roman Empire*, Chap. 2.
9. Bradford, J. 1957. *Ancient landscapes* (London), p. 145.
10. Chatley, H. 1917. "Feng Shui," in *Encyclopaedia Sinica*, ed. by S. Couling (Shanghai), p. 175.
11. *Chou Li*, trans. by E. Biot as *Le Techeou-li* (Paris: 1851) 1:371-74.

12. Mencius, Bk. 1, pt. 1, 3:3.

13. Chen Teng. (1596). Gazetteer. Quoted by W. C. Lowdermilk and D. R. Wickes, *History of soil use in the Wu T'ai Shan area*, Monograph, Royal Asiatic Soc., North China Branch, 1938, p. 8.

14. Wright, A. F. 1965. Symbolism and function: reflections on Changan and other great cities, *J. Asian Studies* 24:670.

15. Mencius, Bk. 3, pt. 1, 4:7.

16. Steward, A. N., and Y. Cheo. 1935. Geographical and ecological notes on botanical exploration in Kwangsi province, China, *Nanking Journal* 5:174.

17. Hartwell, R. 1962. A revolution in Chinese iron and coal industries during the Northern Sung, 960-1126 A.D., *J. Asian Studies* 21:159.

18. Gernet, J. 1962. *Daily life in China on the eve of the Mongol invasion 1250-1276* (London: Allen & Unwin), p. 114.

19. Moule, A. C. 1957. *Quinsai* (Cambridge Univ. Press), p. 51.

20. McMullen, J. 1967. "Confucianism and forestry in seventeenth-century Japan." Unpublished paper, Toronto. I am grateful to Professor McMullen for allowing me to read this.

21. Schafer, E. H. 1962. The conservation of nature under the T'ang dynasty, *J. Econ. and Soc. Hist. of the Orient* 5:299-300.

22. Reischauer, E. O. 1955. *Ennin's travels in T'ang China* (New York: Ronald Press), pp. 153-56.

23. Buchanan, K., 1960. The changing face of rural China, *Pacific Viewpoint* 1:19.

24. Murphey, R. 1967. Man and nature in China, *Modern Asian Studies* 1, no. 4:313-33.

Global Aspect

WHAT FRONTIERS, GEOGRAPHICAL OR POLITICAL, ARE THERE TO THE ENVIRONMENTAL CRISIS?

At what levels of authority must action be taken to insure protection of the earth's biosphere?

To what extent is capitalism—the free-enterprise system—a primary cause of environmental disruption?

How serious are environmental problems in the Soviet Union? In what ways do they differ from those in the United States?

What are the strengths and weaknesses of the socialist system of government in protecting the environment?

The world is undergoing a transformation to which no change that has yet occurred can be compared, either in scope or rapidity.

Charles de Gaulle

. . . . No man is an island entire of itself; every man is a part of the continent, a part of the main. If a clod be washed away by the sea, Europe is the less, as well as if a promontory were, as well as if a manor of thy friend's or of thine own were. Any man's death diminishes me, because I am involved in mankind, and therefore never send to know for whom the bell tolls; it tolls for thee.

John Donne

Mortgaging the
Old Homestead

Lord Ritchie-Calder

Past civilizations are buried in the graveyards of their own mistakes, but as each died of its greed, its carelessness or its effeteness another took its place. That was because such civilizations took their character from a locality or region. Today ours is a global civilization; it is not bounded by the Tigris and the Euphrates nor even the Hellespont and the Indus; it is the whole world. Its planet has shrunk to a neighborhood round which a man-made satellite can patrol 16 times a day, riding the gravitational fences of man's family estate. It is a community so interdependent that our mistakes are exaggerated on a world scale.

For the first time in history, man has the power of veto over the evolution of his own species through a nuclear holocaust. The overkill is enough to wipe out every man, woman and child on earth, together with our fellow lodgers, the animals, the birds and the insects, and to reduce our planet to a radioactive wilderness. Or the Doomsday Machine could be replaced by the Doomsday Bug. By gene manipulation and man-made mutations, it is possible to produce, or generate, a disease against which there would be no natural immunity; by "generate" is meant that even if the perpetrators inoculated themselves protectively, the disease in spreading round the world could assume a virulence of its own and involve them, too. When a British bacteriologist died of the bug he had invented, a distinguished scientist said, "Thank God he didn't sneeze; he could have started a pandemic against which there would have been no immunity."

Modern man can outboast the Ancients, who in the arrogance of their material achievements build pyramids as the gravestones of their civilizations. We can blast our pyramids into space to orbit through all eternity round a planet which perished by our neglect.

A hundred years ago Claude Bernard, the famous French physiologist, enjoined his colleagues, "True science teaches us to doubt and in ignorance to refrain." What he meant was that the scientist must proceed from one tested foothold to the next (like going into a minefield with a mine detector). Today we are using the biosphere, the living space, as an experimental laboratory. When the mad scientist of fiction blows himself and his laboratory skyhigh, that is all right, but when scientists and decision-makers act out of ignorance and pretend that it is knowledge, they are putting the whole world in hazard. Anyway, science at best is not wisdom; it is knowledge, while wisdom is knowledge tempered with judgment. Because of overspecialization, most scientists are disabled from exercising judgments beyond their own sphere.

A classic example was the atomic bomb. It was the Physicists' Bomb. When the device exploded at Alamogordo on July 16, 1945, and made a notch mark in history from which man's future would be dated, the safe-breakers had cracked the lock of the nucleus before the locksmiths knew how it worked. (The evidence of this is the billions of dollars which have been spent since 1945 on gargantuan machines to study the fundamental particles, the components of the nucleus; and they still do not know how they interrelate.)

Prime Minister Clement Attlee, who concurred with President Truman's decision to drop the bomb on Hiroshima, later said: "We knew nothing whatever at that time about the genetic effects of an atomic explosion. I knew nothing about fallout and all the rest of what emerged after Hiroshima. As far as I know, President Truman and Winston Churchill knew nothing of those things either, nor did Sir John Anderson, who coordinated research on our side. Whether the scientists directly concerned knew or guessed, I do not know. But if they did, then so far as I am aware, they said nothing of it to those who had to make the decision."

That sounds absurd, since as long before as 1927, Herman J. Muller had been studying the genetic effects of radiation, work for which he was later awarded the Nobel Prize. But it is true that in the whole documentation of the British effort, before it merged in the Manhattan Project, there is only one reference to genetic effects—a Medical Research Council minute which was not connected with the bomb they were intending to make; it concerned the possibility that the Germans might, short of the bomb, produce radioactive isotopes as a form of biological warfare. In the Franck Report, the most statesmanlike document ever produced by scientists, with its percipience of the military and political consequences of unilateral use of the bomb (presented to Secretary of War Henry L. Stimson even before the test bomb exploded), no reference is made to the biological effects, although one would have supposed that to have been a very powerful argument. The explanation, of course, was that it was the Physicists' Bomb and military security restricted information and discussion to the bomb-makers, which excluded the biologists.

The same kind of breakdown in interdisciplinary consultation was manifest in the subsequent testing of fission and fusion bombs. Categorical assurances were given that the fallout would be confined to the testing area, but the Japanese fishing boat *Lucky Dragon* was "dusted" well outside the predicted range. Then we got the story of radiostrontium. Radiostrontium is an analog of calcium. Therefore in bone-formation an atom of natural strontium can take the place of calcium and the radioactive version can do likewise. For all practical purposes radiostrontium did not exist in the world before 1945; it is a man-made element. Today every young person, anywhere in the world, whose bones were forming during the massive bomb-testing in the atmosphere, carries this brand mark of the Atomic Age. The radiostrontium in their bones is medically insignificant, but, if the test ban (belated recognition) had not prevented the escalation of atmospheric testing, it might not have been.

Every young person everywhere was affected, and why? Because those responsible for H-bomb testing miscalculated. They assumed that the upthrust of the H-bomb would punch a hole in the stratosphere and that the gaseous radioactivity would dissipate itself. One of those gases was radioactive krypton, which quickly decays into radiostrontium, which is a particulate. The technicians had been wrongly briefed about the nature of the troposphere, the climatic ceiling which would, they maintained, prevent the fallback. But between the equatorial troposphere and the polar troposphere there is a gap, and the radiostrontium came back through this fanlight into the climatic jet streams. It was swept all round the world to come to earth as radioactive rain, to be deposited on food crops and pastures, to be ingested by animals and to get into milk and into babies and children and adolescents whose growing bones were hungry for calcium or its equivalent strontium, in this case radioactive. Incidentally, radiostrontium was known to the biologists before it "hit the headlines." They had found it in the skin burns of animals exposed on the Nevada testing ranges and they knew its sinister nature as a "bone-seeker." But the authorities clapped security on their work, classified it as "Operation Sunshine" and cynically called the units of radiostrontium "Sunshine Units"—an instance not of ignorance but of deliberate noncommunication.

One beneficial effect of the alarm caused by all this has been that the atoms industry is, bar none, the safest in the world for those working in it. Precautions, now universal, were built into the code of practice from the beginning.

Indeed it can be admitted that the safety margins in health and in working conditions are perhaps excessive in the light of experience, but no one would dare to modify them. There can, however, be accidents in which the public assumes the risk. At Windscale, the British atomic center in Cumberland, a reactor burned out. Radioactive fumes escaped from the stacks in spite of the filters. They drifted over the country. Milk was dumped into the sea because radioactive iodine had covered the dairy pastures.

There is the problem of atomic waste disposal, which persists in the peaceful uses as well as in the making of nuclear explosives. Low energy wastes, carefully monitored, can be safely disposed of. Trash, irradiated metals and laboratory waste can be embedded in concrete and dumped in the ocean deeps—although this practice raises some misgivings. But high-level wastes, some with elements the radioactivity of which can persist for hundreds of thousands of years, present prodigious difficulties. There must be "burial grounds" (or, euphemistically, "farms"), the biggest of which is at Hanford, Wash. The Hanford "farm" encloses a stretch of the Columbia River in a tract covering 575 square miles where no one is allowed to live or to trespass.

There, in the 20th-century Giza, it has cost more, much more, to bury live atoms than it cost to entomb the sun-god kings of Egypt. The capital outlay runs into hundreds of millions of dollars and the maintenance of the U.S. sepulchers is more than $6 million a year. (Add to that the buried waste of the U.S.S.R., Britain, Canada, France and China, and one can see what it costs to bury live atoms.) And they are very much alive. At Hanford they are kept in million-gallon carbon-steel tanks. Their radioactive vitality keeps the accompanying acids boiling like a witch's cauldron. A cooling system has to be maintained continuously. The vapors from the self-boiling tanks have to be condensed and "scrubbed" (radioactive atoms removed); otherwise a radioactive miasma would escape from the vents. The tanks will not endure as long as the pyramids and certainly not for the hundreds of thousands of years of the long-lived atoms. The acids and the atomic ferments erode the toughest metal, so the tanks have to be periodically decanted. Another method is to entomb them in disused salt mines. Another is to embed them in ceramics, lock them up in glass beads. Another is what is known as "hydraulic fraction": a hole is drilled into a shale formation (below the subsoil water); liquid is piped down under pressure and causes the shale to split laterally. Hence the atoms in liquid cement can be injected under enormous pressure and spread into the fissures to set like a radioactive sandwich.

This accumulating waste from fission plants will persist until the promise, still far from fulfilled, of peaceful thermonuclear power comes about. With the multiplication of power reactors, the wastes will increase. It is calculated that by the year 2000, the number of six-ton nuclear "hearses" in transit to "burial grounds" at any given time on the highways of the United States will be well over 3,000 and the amount of radioactive products will be about a billion curies, which is a mighty lot of curies to be roaming around a populated country.

The alarming possibilities were well illustrated by the incident at Palomares on the coast of Spain, when there occurred a collision of a refueling aircraft with a U.S. nuclear bomber on "live" mission. The bombs were scattered. There was no explosion, but radioactive materials broke loose and contaminated beaches and farm soil had to be scooped up and taken to the United States for burial.

Imagine what would have happened if the *Torrey Canyon*, the giant tanker which was wrecked off the Scilly Isles, had been nuclear-powered. Some experts make comforting noises and say that the reactors would have "closed down," but the *Torrey Canyon* was a wreck and the Palomares incident showed what happens when radioactive materials break loose. All those oil-polluted beaches of southwest England and the coasts of Brittany would have had to be scooped up for nuclear burial.

The *Torrey Canyon* is a nightmarish example of progress for its own sake. The bigger the tanker, the cheaper the freightage, which is supposed to be progress. This ship was built at Newport News, Va. in 1959 for the Union Oil Company; it was a giant for the time—810 feet long and 104 feet beam—but, five years later, that was not big enough. She was taken to Japan to be "stretched." The ship was cut in half amidship and a mid-body section inserted. With a new bow, this made her 974 feet long, and her beam was extended 21 feet. She could carry 850,000 barrels of oil, twice her original capacity.

Built for Union Oil, she was "owned" by the Barracuda Tanker Corporation, the head office of which is a filing cabinet in Hamilton, Bermuda. She was registered under the Liberian flag of convenience and her captain and crew were Italians recruited in Genoa. Just to complicate the international tangle, she was under charter to the British Petroleum Tanker Company to bring 118,000 tons of crude oil from Kuwait to Milford Haven in Wales, via the Cape of Good Hope. Approaching Lands End, the Italian captain was informed that if he did not reach Milford Haven by 11 p.m. Saturday night he would miss high water and would not be able to enter the harbor for another five days, which would have annoyed his employers. He took a shortcut, setting course between Seven Stones rocks and the Scilly Isles, and he finished up on Pollard Rock, in an area where no ship of that size should ever have been.

Her ruptured tanks began to vomit oil and great slicks appeared over the sea in the direction of the Cornish holiday beaches. A Dutch tug made a dash for the stranded ship, gambling on the salvage money. (Where the salvaged ship could have been taken one cannot imagine, since no place would offer harborage to a leaking tanker.) After delays and a death in the futile salvage effort, the British Government moved in with the navy, the air force and, on the beaches, the army. They tried to set fire to the floating oil which, of course, would not volatilize. They covered the slicks with detergents (supplied at a price by the oil companies), and then the bombers moved in to try to cut open the deck and, with incendiaries, to set fire to the remaining oil in the tanks. Finally the ship foundered and divers confirmed that the oil had been effectively consumed.

Nevertheless the result was havoc. All measures had had to be improvised. Twelve thousand tons of detergent went into the sea. Later marine biologists found that the cure had been worse than the complaint. The oil was disastrous for seabirds, but marine organic life was destroyed by the detergents. By arduous physical efforts, with bulldozers and flamethrowers and, again, more detergents, the beaches were cleaned up for the holiday-makers. Northerly winds swept the oil slicks down Channel to the French coast with even more serious consequences, particularly to the valuable shellfish industry. With even bigger tankers being launched, this affair is a portentous warning.

Two years after *Torrey Canyon,* an offshore oil rig erupted in the Santa Barbara Channel. The disaster to wildlife in this area, which has island nature reserves and is on the migratory route of whales, seals and seabirds, was a repetition of the *Torrey Canyon* oil spill. And the operator of the lethal oil rig was Union Oil.

Another piece of stupidity shows how much we are at the mercy of ignorant men pretending to be knowledgeable. During the International Geophysical Year, 1957-58, the Van Allen Belt was discovered. This is an area of magnetic phenomena. Immediately it was decided to explode a nuclear bomb in the belt to see whether an artificial aurora could be produced. The colorful draperies and luminous skirts of the aurora borealis are caused by the drawing in of cosmic particles through the rare gases of the upper atmosphere— ionization it is called; it is like passing electrons through the vacuum tubes of our familiar fluorescent lighting. The name Rainbow Bomb was given it in anticipation of the display it was expected to produce. Every eminent scientist in the field of cosmology, radio astronomy or physics of the atmosphere protested at this irresponsible tampering with a system which we did not understand. And, typical of the casual attitude toward this kind of thing, the Prime Minister of the day, answering protests in the House of Commons that called on him to intervene with the Americans, asked what all the fuss was about. After all, they hadn't known that the Van Allen Belt even existed a year before. This was the cosmic equivalent of Chamberlain's remark about Czechoslovakia, at the time of Munich, about that distant country of which we knew so little. They exploded the bomb. They got their pyrotechnics and we still do not know the cost we may have to pay for this artificial magnetic disturbance.

In the same way we can look with misgivings on those tracks—the white tails of the jets that are introducing into our climatic system new factors, the effects of which are immensurable. Formation of rain clouds depends upon water vapor having a nucleus on which to form. That is how artificial precipitation is introduced—the so-called rain-making. So the jets, crisscrossing the weather system, playing noughts and crosses with it, can produce a man-made change.

In the longer term we can foresee even more drastic effects from man's unthinking operations. At the United Nations' Science and Technology Conference in Geneva in 1963 we took stock of the effects of industrialization on our total environment thus far. The atmosphere is not only the air which humans, animals and plants breathe, it is also the envelope that protects living things from harmful radiation from the sun and outer space. It is also the medium of climate, the winds and the rain. Those are inseparable from the hydrosphere—the oceans, covering seven-tenths of the globe, with their currents and extraordinary rates of evaporation; the biosphere, with its trees and their transpiration; and, in terms of human activities, the minerals mined from the lithosphere, the rock crust. Millions of years ago the sun encouraged the growth of the primeval forests, which became our coal, and the plant growth of the seas, which became our oil. Those fossil fuels, locked away for eons of time, are extracted by man and put back into the atmosphere from the chimney stacks and the exhaust pipes of modern engineering. About six billion tons of carbon are mixed with the atmosphere annually. During the past century, in the process of industrialization, with its release of carbon by the burning of fossil fuels, more than 400 billion tons of carbon have been artificially introduced into the atmosphere. The concentration in the air we breathe has been increased approximately 10%, and if all the known reserves of coal and oil were burned at once the concentration would be 10 times greater.

This is something more than a public health problem, more than a question of what goes into the lungs of an individual, more than a question of smog. The carbon cycle in nature is a self-adjusting mechanism. Carbon dioxide is, of course, indispensable for plants and is, therefore, a source of life, but there is a balance which is maintained by excess carbon being absorbed by the seas. The excess is now taxing this absorption, and it can seriously disturb the heat balance of the earth because of what is known as the "greenhouse effect." A greenhouse lets in the sun's rays but retains the heat. Carbon dioxide, as a transparent diffusion, does likewise. It keeps the heat at the surface of the earth and in excess modifies the climate.

It has been estimated that, at the present rate of increase, the mean annual temperature all over the world might increase by 3.6° centigrade in the next 40 to 50 years. The experts may argue about the time factor and even about the effects, but certain things are apparent, not only in the industrialized northern hemisphere but in the southern hemisphere also. The north-polar ice cap is thinning and shrinking. The seas, with their blanket of carbon dioxide, are changing their temperature, with the result that marine plant life is increasing and is transpiring more carbon dioxide. As a result of the combination, fish are migrating, changing even their latitudes. On land the snow line is retreating and glaciers are melting. In Scandinavia, land which was perennially under snow and ice is thawing, and arrowheads of more than 1,000 years ago, when the black soils were last exposed, have been found. The melting of sea ice will not affect the sea level, because the volume of floating ice is the same as the water it displaces, but the melting of ice caps or glaciers, in which the water is locked up, will introduce additional water to the sea and raise the level. Rivers originating in glaciers and permanent snow fields will increase their flow; and if ice dams, such as those in the Himalayas, break, the results in flooding may be catastrophic. In this process the patterns of rainfall will change, with increased precipitation in some areas and the possibility of aridity in now fertile regions. One would be well advised not to take 99-year leases on properties at present sea level.

At that same conference, there was a sobering reminder of mistakes which can be writ large, from the very best intentions. In the Indus Valley in West Pakistan, the population is increasing at the rate of 10 more mouths to be fed every five minutes. In that same five minutes in that same place, an acre of land is being lost through waterlogging and salinity. This is the largest irrigated region in the world. Twenty-three million acres are artificially watered by canals. The Indus and its tributaries, the Jhelum, the Chenab, the Ravi, the Beas and the Sutlej, created the alluvial plains of the Punjab and the Sind. In the 19th century, the British began a big program of farm development in lands which were fertile but had low rainfall. Barrages and distribution canals were constructed. One thing which, for economy's sake, was not done was to line the canals. In the early days, this genuinely did not matter. The water was being spread from the Indus into a thirsty plain and if it soaked in so much the better. The system also depended on what is called "inland delta drainage," that is to say, the water spreads out like a delta and then drains itself back into the river. After independence, Pakistan, with external aid, started vigorously to extend the Indus irrigation. The experts all said the soil was good and would produce abundantly once it got the distributed water. There were plenty of experts, but they all overlooked one thing—the hydrological imperatives. The incline from Lahore to the Rann of Kutch—700 miles— is a foot a mile, a quite inadequate drainage gradient. So as more and more barrages and more and more lateral canals were built, the water was not draining back into the Indus. Some 40% of the water in the unlined canals seeped underground, and in a network of 40,000 miles of canals that is a lot of water. The result was that the water table rose. Low-lying areas became waterlogged, drowning the roots of the crops. In other areas the water crept upward, leaching salts that accumulated in the surface layers, poisoning the crops. At the same time the irrigation regime, which used just 1½ inches of water a year in the fields, did not sluice out those salts but added, through evaporation, its own salts. The result was tragically spectacular. In flying over large tracts of this area, one would imagine that it was an Arctic landscape because the white crust of salt glistens like snow.

The situation was deteriorating so rapidly that President Ayub appealed in person to President Kennedy, who sent out a high-powered mission which encompassed 20 disciplines. This was backed by the computers at Harvard. The answers were pretty grim. It would take 20 years and $2 billion to repair the damage—more than it cost to create the installations that did the damage. It would mean using vertical drainage to bring up the water and use it for irrigation, and also to sluice out the salt in the surface soil. If those 20 scientific disciplines had been brought together in the first instance, it would not have happened.

One more instance of the far-flung consequences of man's localized mistakes: no insecticides or pesticides have ever been allowed into the continent of Antarctica. Yet they have been found in the fauna along the northern coasts. They have come almost certainly from the northern hemisphere, carried from the rivers of the farm states into the currents sweeping south. In November 1969, the U.S. Government decided to "phase out" the use of DDT.

Pollution is a crime compounded of ignorance and avarice. The great achievements of *Homo sapiens* become the disaster-ridden blunders of unthinking man—poisoned rivers and dead lakes, polluted with the effluents of industries which give something called "prosperity" at the expense of posterity. Rivers are treated like sewers and lakes like cesspools. These natural systems—and they are living systems—have struggled hard. The benevolent micro-organisms which cope with reasonable amounts of organic matter have been destroyed by mineral detergents. Witness our foaming streams. Lake Erie did its best to provide the oxygen to neutralize the pickling acids of the great steelworks. But it could not contend. It lost its oxygen in the battle. Its once rich commercial fishing industry died and its revitalizing micro-organic life gave place to anaerobic organisms which do not need oxygen but give off foul smells, the mortuary smells of dead water. As one Erie industrialist retorted, "It's not our effluent; it's those damned dead fish."

We have had the Freedom from Hunger Campaign; presently we shall need a Freedom from Thirst Campaign. If the International Hydrological Decade does not bring us to our senses, we will face a desperate situation. Of course it is bound up with the increasing population, but also with the extravagances of the technologies which claim that they are serving that population. There is a competition between the water needs of the land which has to feed the increasing population and the domestic and industrial needs of that population. The theoretical minimum to sustain living standards is about 300 gallons a day per person. This is the approximate amount of water needed to produce grain for 2½ pounds of bread, but a diet of two pounds of bread and one pound of beef would require about 2,500 gallons. And that is nothing compared with the gluttonous requirements of steel-making, paper-making and the chemical industry.

Water—just H_2O—is as indispensable as food. To die of hunger one needs more than 15 days. To die of thirst one needs only three. Yet we are squandering, polluting and destroying water. In Los Angeles and neighboring Southern California, a thousand times more water is being consumed than is being precipitated in the locality. They have preempted the water of neighboring states. They are piping it from Northern California, and there is a plan to pipe it all the way from Canada's Northwest Territories, from the Mackenzie and the Liard, which flow northward to the Arctic Ocean, to turn them back into deserts.

Always and everywhere we come back to the problem of population—more people to make more mistakes, more people to be the victims of the mistakes of others, more people to suffer hell upon earth. It is appalling to hear people complacently talking about the population explosion as though it belonged to the future, or world hunger as though it were threatening, when hundreds of millions can testify that it is already here—swear it with panting breath.

We know to the exact countdown second when the nuclear explosion took place—5:30 a.m., July 16, 1945, when the first device went off in the desert of Alamogordo, N. Mex. The fuse of the population explosion had been lit 10 years earlier—February 1935. On that day a girl called Hildegarde was dying of generalized septicemia. She had pricked her finger with a sewing needle and the infection had run amok. The doctors could not save her. Her desperate father injected a red dye into her body. Her father was Gerhard Domagk. The red dye was prontosil, which he, a pharmaceutical chemist, had produced and had successfully used on mice lethally infected with streptococci, but never before on a human. Prontosil was the first of the sulfa drugs—chemotherapeutics—which could attack the germ within the living body. Thus was prepared the way for the rediscovery of penicillin—rediscovery because, although Fleming had discovered it in 1928, it had been ignored; neither he nor anybody else had seen its supreme virtue of attacking germs within the living body. That is the operative phrase, for while medical science and the medical profession had used antiseptics for surface wounds and sores, they were always labeled "Poison, not to be taken internally." The sulfa drugs had shown that it was possible to attack specific germs within the living body and had changed this attitude. So when Chain and Florey looked again at Fleming's penicillin in 1938, they were seeing it in the light of the experience of the sulfas.

A new era of disease-fighting had begun—the sulfas, the antibiotics, DDT insecticides. Doctors could now attack a whole range of invisible enemies. They could master the old killer diseases. They proved it during the war, and when the war ended there were not only stockpiles of the drugs, there were tooled-up factories to produce them. So, to prevent the spread of the deadly epidemics which follow wars, the supplies were made available to the war-ravaged countries with their displaced persons, and then to the developing countries. Their indigenous infections and contagions and insect-borne diseases were checked.

Almost symbolically, the first great clinical use of prontosil had been in dealing with puerperal sepsis, childbed fever. It had spectacularly saved mothers' lives in Queen Charlotte's Hospital, London. Now its successors took up the story. Fewer mothers died in childbirth, to live and have more babies. Fewer infants died, fewer toddlers, fewer adolescents. They lived to marry and have children. Older people were not killed off by, for instance, malaria. The average life-span increased.

Professor Kingsley Davis of the University of California at Berkeley, the authority on urban development, has presented a hair-raising picture from his survey of the world's cities. He has shown that 38% of the world's population is already living in what are defined as urban places. More than one-fifth of the world's population is living in cities of 100,000 or more. And more than one-tenth of the world's population is now living in cities of a million or more inhabitants. In 1968, 375 million people were living in million-and-over cities. The proportions are changing so quickly that on present trends it would take only 16 years for half the world's population to be living in cities and only 55 years for it to reach 100%.

Within the lifetime of a child born today, Kingsley Davis foresees, on present trends of population increase, 15 billion people to be fed and housed—nearly five times as many as now. The whole human species would be living in cities of a million and over inhabitants, and—wait for it!—the biggest city would have 1.3 billion inhabitants. That means 186 times as many as there are in Greater London.

For years the Greek architect Doxiadis has been warning us about such prospects. In his Ecumenopolis—World City—one urban area would ooze into the next, like confluent ulcers. The East Side of World City would have as its High Street the Eurasian Highway stretching from Glasgow to Bangkok, with the Channel Tunnel as its subway and a built-up area all the way. On the West Side of World City, divided not by the tracks but by the Atlantic, the pattern is already emerging, or rather, merging. Americans already talk about Boswash, the urban development of a built-up area stretching from Boston to Washington; and on the West Coast, apart from Los Angeles sprawling into the desert, the realtors are already slurring one city into another all along the Pacific Coast from the Mexican border to San Francisco. We don't need a crystal ball to foresee what Davis and Doxiadis are predicting; we can already see it through smog-covered spectacles. A blind man can smell what is coming.

The danger of prediction is that experts and men of affairs are likely to plan for the predicted trends and confirm these trends. "Prognosis" is something different from "Prediction." An intelligent doctor, having diagnosed your symptoms and examined your condition, does not say (except in novelettes), "You have six months to live." An intelligent doctor says, "Frankly, your condition is serious. Unless you do so-and-so, it is bound to deteriorate." The operative phrase is "do so-and-so." We don't have to plan for trends; if they are socially undesirable our duty is to plan away from them, to treat the symptoms before they become malignant.

We have to do this on the local, the national and the international scale, through intergovernmental action, because there are no frontiers in present-day pollution and destruction of the biosphere. Mankind shares a common habitat. We have mortgaged the old homestead and Nature is liable to foreclose.

The truth, the central stupendous truth, about developed countries today is that they can have—in anything but the shortest run—the kind and scale of resources they decide to have. . . . It is no longer resources that limit decisions. It is the decision that makes the resources. This is the fundamental revolutionary change—perhaps the most revolutionary mankind has ever known.

U Thant

Today, in our country and in certain other industrial nations, men are compelled to recognize and give assent to profound transformations in human values. . . . The citizens and the institutions of these nations must accommodate themselves to the law of material abundance; each individual can secure increase in his own well-being only through action that secures increase in the well-being of others.

Gerard Piel

The Convergence
of Environmental
Disruption
Marshall I. Goldman

By now it is a familiar story: rivers that blaze with fire, smog that suffocates cities, streams that vomit dead fish, oil slicks that blacken seacoasts, prized beaches that vanish in the waves, and lakes that evaporate and die a slow smelly death. What makes it unfamiliar is that this is a description not only of the United States but also of the Soviet Union.

Most conservationists and social critics are unaware that the U.S.S.R. has environmental disruption that is as extensive and severe as ours. Most of us have been so distressed by our own environmental disruption that we lack the emotional energy to worry about anyone else's difficulties. Yet, before we can find a solution to the environmental disruption in our own country, it is necessary to explain why it is that a socialist or communist country like the U.S.S.R. finds itself abusing the environment in the same way, and to the same degree, that we abuse it. This is especially important for those who have come to believe as basic doctrine that it is capitalism and private greed that are the root cause of environmental disruption. Undoubtedly private enterprise and the profit motive account for a good portion of the environmental disruption that we encounter in this country. However, a study of pollution in the Soviet Union suggests that abolishing private property will not necessarily mean an end to environmental disruption. In some ways, state ownership of the country's productive resources may actually exacerbate rather than ameliorate the situation.

THE PUBLIC GOOD

That environmental disruption is a serious matter in the Soviet Union usually comes as a surprise not only to most radical critics of pollution in the West but also to many Russians. It has been assumed that, if all the factories in a society were state-owned, the state would insure that the broader interests of the general public would be protected. Each factory would be expected to bear the full costs and consequences of its operation. No factory would be allowed to take a particular action if it meant that the public would suffer or would have to bear the expense. In other words, the factory would not only have to pay for its *private costs*, such as expenses for labor and raw materials; it would also have to pay for its *social costs*, such as the cost of eliminating the air and water pollution it had caused. It was argued that, since the industry was state-run, including both types of costs would not be difficult. At least that was what was assumed.

Soviet officials continue today to make such assumptions. B. V. Petrovsky, the Soviet Minister of Public Health, finds environmental disruption in a capitalist society perfectly understandable: "the capitalist system by its very essence is incapable of taking radical measures to ensure the efficient conservation of nature." By implication he assumed that the Soviet Union can take such measures. Therefore it must be somewhat embarrassing for Nikolai Popov, an editor of *Soviet Life*, to have to ask, "Why, in a socialist country, whose constitution explicitly says the public interest may not be ignored with impunity, are industry executives permitted to break the laws protecting nature?"

Behind Popov's questions is a chronicle of environmental disruption that is as serious as almost any that exists in the world. Of course in a country as large as the U.S.S.R. there are many places that have been spared man's disruptive incursions. But, as the population grows in numbers and mobility, such areas become fewer and fewer. Moreover, as in the United States, the most idyllic sites are the very ones that tend to attract the Soviet population.

Just because human beings intrude on an area, it does not necessarily follow that the area's resources will be abused. Certainly the presence of human beings means some alteration in the previous ecological balance, and in some cases there may be severe damage, but the change need not be a serious one. Nonetheless, many of the changes that have taken place in the Soviet Union have been major ones. As a result, the quality of the air, water, and land resources has been adversely affected.

WATER

Comparing pollution in the United States and in the U.S.S.R. is something like a game. Any depressing story that can be told about an incident in the United States can be matched by a horror story from the U.S.S.R. For example, there have been hundreds of fish-kill incidents in both countries. Rivers and lakes from Maine to California have had such incidents. In the U.S.S.R., effluent from the Chernorechensk Chemical Plant near Dzerzhinsk killed almost all the fish life in the Oka River in 1965 because of uncontrolled dumping. Factories along major rivers such as the Volga, Ob, Yenesei, Ural, and Northern Dvina have committed similar offenses, and these rivers are considered to be highly polluted. There is not one river in the Ukraine whose natural state has been preserved (1). The Molognaia River in the Ukraine and many other rivers throughout the country are officially reported as dead. How dangerous this can be is illustrated by what happened in Sverdlovsk in 1965. A careless smoker threw his cigarette into the Iset River and, like the Cuyahoga in Cleveland, the Iset caught fire.

Sixty-five percent of all the factories in the largest Soviet republic, the Russian Soviet Federated Socialist Republic (RSFSR), discharge their waste without bothering to clean it up *(2)*. But factories are not the only ones responsible for the poor quality of the water. Mines, oil wells, and ships freely dump their waste and ballast into the nearest body of water. Added to this industrial waste is the sewage of many Russian cities. Large cities like Moscow and Leningrad are struggling valiantly, like New York and Chicago, to treat their waste, but many municipalities are hopelessly behind in their efforts to do the job properly. Only six out of the 20 main cities in Moldavia have a sewer system, and only two of those cities make any effort to treat their sewage *(3)*. Similarly, only 40 percent of the cities and suburbs in the RSFSR have any equipment for treating their sewage. For that matter, according to the last completed census, taken in 1960, only 35 percent of all the housing units in urban areas are served by a sewer system *(4)*.

Conditions are even more primitive in the countryside. Often this adversely affects the well-water and groundwater supplies, especially in areas of heavy population concentration. Under the circumstances it is not surprising to find that major cities like Vladimir, Orenburg, and Voronezh do not have adequate supplies of drinking water. In one instance reported in *Pravda,* a lead and zinc ore enriching plant was built in 1966 and allowed to dump its wastes in the Fragdon River, even though the river was the sole source of water for about 40 kilometers along its route. As a result the water became contaminated and many people were simply left without anything to drink.

Even when there are supplies of pure water, many homes throughout the country are not provided with running water. This was true of 62 percent of the urban residences in the U.S.S.R. in 1960 *(4)*. The Russians often try to explain this by pointing to the devastation they suffered during World War II. Still it is something of a shock, 25 years after the war, to walk along one of the more fashionable streets in Kharkov, the fifth largest city in the U.S.S.R., and see many of the area's residents with a yoke across their shoulders, carrying two buckets of water. The scene can be duplicated in almost any other city in the U.S.S.R.

Again, the Soviet Union, like the United States, has had trouble not only with its rivers but with its larger bodies of water. As on Cape Cod and along the California coast, oil from slicks has coated the shores of the Baltic, Black, and Caspian seas. Refineries and tankers have been especially lax in their choice of oil-disposal procedures.

Occasionally it is not only the quality but the quantity of the water that causes concern. The Aral and Caspian seas have been gradually disappearing. Because both seas are in arid regions, large quantities of their water have been diverted for crop irrigation. Moreover, many dams and reservoirs have been built on the rivers that supply both seas for the generation of electric power. As a result of such activities, the Aral Sea began to disappear. From 1961 to 1969 its surface dropped 1 to 3 meters. Since the average depth of the sea is only about 20 to 30 meters, some Russian authorities fear that, at the current rate of shrinkage, by the turn of the century the sea will be nothing but a salt marsh (5).

Similarly, during the past 20 years the level of the Caspian Sea has fallen almost 2½ meters. This has drastically affected the sea's fish population. Many of the best spawning areas have turned into dry land. For the sturgeon, one of the most important fish in the Caspian, this has meant the elimination of one-third of the spawning area. The combined effect of the oil on the sea and the smaller spawning area reduced the fish catch in the Caspian from 1,180,400 centners in 1942 to 586,300 centners in 1966. Food fanciers are worried not so much about the sturgeon as about the caviar that the sturgeon produces. The output of caviar has fallen even more drastically than the sea level—a concern not only for the Russian consumers of caviar but for foreigners. Caviar had been a major earner of foreign exchange. Conditions have become so serious that the Russians have now begun to experiment with the production of artificial caviar.

The disruption of natural life in the Caspian Sea has had some serious ecological side effects. Near Ashkhabad at the mouth of the Volga a fish called the belyi amur also began to disappear. As a consequence, the mosquito population, which had been held in check by the belyi amur, grew in the newly formed swamps where once the sea had been. In turn, the mosquitoes began to transmit malaria (6).

Perhaps the best known example of the misuse of water resources in the U.S.S.R. has been what happened to Lake Baikal. This magnificent lake is estimated to be over 20 million years old. There are over 1200 species of living organisms in the lake, including freshwater seals and 700 other organisms that are found in few or no other places in the world. It is one of the largest and deepest freshwater lakes on earth, over 1½ kilometers deep in some areas (7). It is five times as deep as Lake Superior and contains twice the volume of water. In fact, Lake Baikal holds almost one-fortieth of all the world's fresh water. The water is low in salt content and is highly transparent; one can see as far as 36 meters under water (8).

In 1966, first one and then another paper and pulp mill appeared on Lake Baikal's shores. Immediately limnologists and conservationists protested this assault on an international treasure. Nonetheless, new homes were built in the vicinity of the paper and pulp mills, and the plant at the nearby town of Baikalsk began to dump 60 million cubic meters of effluent a year into the lake. A specially designed treatment plant had been erected in the hope that it would maintain the purity of the lake. Given the unique quality of the water, however, it soon became apparent that almost no treatment plant would be good enough. Even though the processed water is drinkable, it still has a yellowish tinge and a barely perceptible odor. As might be expected, a few months after this effluent had been discharged into the lake, the Limnological Institute reported that animal and plant life had decreased by one-third to one-half in the zone where the sewage was being discharged.

Several limnologists have argued that the only effective way to prevent the mill's effluent from damaging the lake is to keep it out of the lake entirely. They suggest that this can be done if a 67-kilometer sewage conduit is built over the mountains to the Irkut River, which does not flow into the lake. So far the Ministry of Paper and Pulp Industries has strongly opposed this, since it would cost close to $40 million to build such a bypass. They argue that they have already spent a large sum on preventing pollution. Part of their lack of enthusiasm for any further change may also be explained by the fact that they have only had to pay fines of $55 for each violation. It has been cheaper to pay the fines than to worry about a substantial cleanup operation.

Amid continuing complaints, the second paper and pulp mill, at Kamensk, was told that it must build and test its treatment plant before production of paper and pulp would be allowed. Moreover, the lake and its entire drainage basin have been declared a "protected zone," which means that in the future all timber cutting and plant operations are to be strictly regulated. Many critics, however, doubt the effectiveness of such orders. As far back as 1960, similar regulations were issued for Lake Baikal and its timber, without much result. In addition, the Ministry of Pulp and Paper Industries has plans for constructing yet more paper and pulp mills along the shores of Lake Baikal and is lobbying for funds to build them.

Many ecologists fear that, even if no more paper mills are built, the damage may already have been done. The construction of the mills and towns necessitated the cutting of trees near the shoreline, which inevitably increased the flow of silt into the lake and its feeder streams. Furthermore, instead of being shipped by rail, as was originally promised, the logs are rafted on the water to the mill for processing. Unfortunately about 10 percent of these logs sink to the lake bottom in transit. Not only does this cut off the feeding and breeding grounds on the bottom of the lake but the logs consume the lake's oxygen, which again reduces its purity.

There are those who see even more dire consequences from the exploitation of the timber around the lake. The Gobi Desert is just over the border in Mongolia. The cutting of the trees and the intrusion of machinery into the wooded areas has destroyed an important soil stabilizer. Many scientists report that the dunes have already started to move, and some fear that the Gobi Desert will sweep into Siberia and destroy the taiga and the lake.

AIR

The misuse of air resources in the U.S.S.R. is not very different from the misuse of water. Despite the fact that the Russians at present produce less than one-tenth the number of cars each year that we produce in the United States, most Soviet cities have air pollution. It can be quite serious, especially when the city is situated in a valley or a hilly region. In the hilly cities of Armenia, the established health norms for carbon monoxide are often exceeded. Similarly Magnitogorsk, Alma Ata, and Chelyabinsk, with their metallurgical industries, frequently have a dark blue cap over them. Like Los Angeles, Tbilisi, the capital of the Republic of Georgia, has smog almost 6 months of the year. Nor is air pollution limited to hilly regions. Leningrad has 40 percent fewer clear daylight hours than the nearby town of Pavlovsk (9).

Of all the factories that emit harmful wastes through their stacks, only 14 percent were reported in 1968 to have fully equipped air-cleaning devices. Another 26 percent had some treatment equipment. Even so, there are frequent complaints that such equipment is either operating improperly or of no use. There have been several reported instances of factories' spewing lead into the air (10). In other cases, especially in Sverdlovsk and Magnitogorsk, public health officials ordered the closing of factories and boilers. Nevertheless, there are periodic complaints that some public health officials have yielded to the pleadings and pressures of factory directors and have agreed to keep the plants open "on a temporary basis."

One particularly poignant instance of air pollution is occurring outside the historic city of Tula. Not far away is the site of Leo Tolstoy's former summer estate, Yasnaya Polyana, now an internationally known tourist attraction with lovely grounds and a museum. Due to some inexcusable oversight, a small coal-gasification plant was built within view of Yasnaya Polyana in 1955. In 1960 the plant was expanded as it began to produce fertilizer and other chemicals. Now known as the Shchkino Chemical Complex, the plant has over 6000 employees and produces a whole range of chemicals, including formaldehyde and synthetic fibers. Unfortunately the prevailing winds from this extensive complex blow across the street onto the magnificent forests at Yasnaya Polyana. As a result, a prime oak forest is reported near extinction and a pine forest is similarly affected.

LAND

As in other nations of the world, environmental disruption in the U.S.S.R. is not limited to air and water. For example, the Black Sea coast in the Soviet Republic of Georgia is disappearing. Since this is a particularly desirable resort area, a good deal of concern has been expressed over what is happening. At some places the sea has moved as much as 40 meters inland. Near the resort area of Adler, hospitals, resort hotels, and (of all things) the beach sanitarium of the Ministry of Defense collapsed as the shoreline gave way. Particular fears that the mainline railway will also be washed away shortly have been expressed.

New Yorkers who vacation on Fire Island have had comparable difficulties, but the cause of the erosion in the U.S.S.R.

is unique. Excessive construction has loosened the soil (as at Fire Island) and accelerated the process of erosion. But, in addition, much of the Black Sea area has been simply hauled away by contractors. One contractor realized that the pebbles and sand on the riviera-type beach were a cheap source of gravel. Soon many contractors were taking advantage of nature's blessings. As a result, as much as 120,000 cubic meters a year of beach material has been hauled away. Unfortunately the natural process by which those pebbles are replaced was disrupted when the state came along and built a network of dams and reservoirs on the stream feeding into the sea. This provided a source of power and water but it stopped the natural flow of pebbles and sand to the seacoast. Without the pebbles, there is little to cushion the enormous power of the waves as they crash against the coast and erode the shoreline.

In an effort to curb the erosion, orders have been issued to prevent the construction of any more buildings within 3 kilometers of the shore. Concrete piers have also been constructed to absorb the impact of the waves, and efforts are being made to haul gravel material from the inland mountains to replace that which has been taken from the seacoast. Still the contractors are disregarding the orders—they continue to haul away the pebbles and sand, and the seacoast continues to disappear.

Nor is the Black Sea coast the only instance of such disregard for the forces of nature. High in the Caucasus is the popular health resort and spa of Kislovodsk. Surrounded on three sides by a protective semicircle of mountains which keep out the cold winds of winter, the resort has long been noted for its unique climate and fresh mountain air. Whereas Kislovodsk used to have 311 days of sun a year, Piatagorsk on the other side of the mountain had only 122 *(11)*. Then, shortly after World War II, an official of the Ministry of Railroads sought to increase the volume of railroad freight in the area. He arranged for the construction of a lime kiln in the nearby village of Podkumok. With time, pressure mounted to increase the processing of lime, so that now there are eight kilns in operation. As the manager of the lime kiln operation and rail-road officials continued to "fulfill their ever-increasing plan" in the name of "socialist competition," the mountain barrier protecting Kislovodsk from the northern winds and smoke of the lime kilns has been gradually chopped away. Conse-quently, Kislovodsk has almost been transformed into an ordinary industrial city. The dust in the air now exceeds by 50 percent the norm for a *nonresort* city.

Much as some of our ecologists have been warning that we are on the verge of some fundamental disruptions of nature, so the Russians have their prophets of catastrophe. Several geographers and scientists have become especially concerned about the network of hydroelectric stations and irrigation reservoirs and canals that have been built with great fanfare across the country. They are now beginning to find that such projects have had several unanticipated side effects. For example, because the irrigation canals have not been lined, there has been considerable seepage of water. The seepage from the canals and an overenthusiastic use of water for irri-gation has caused a rise in the water table in many areas. This has facilitated salination of the soil, especially in dry areas. Similarly, the damming of water bodies apparently has dis-rupted the addition of water to underground water reserves. There is concern that age-old sources of drinking water may gradually disappear. Finally, it is feared that the reduction of old water surfaces and the formation of new ones has radically altered and increased the amount of water evaporation in the area in question. There is evidence that this has brought about a restructuring of old climate and moisture patterns *(12)*. This may mean the formation of new deserts in the area. More worrisome is the possibility of an extension of the ice cap. If enough of Russia's northward-flowing rivers are diverted for irrigation purposes to the arid south, this will deprive the Arctic Ocean of the warmer waters it receives from these rivers. Some scientist critics also warn that reversing the flow of some of the world's rivers in this way will have disruptive effects on the rotation of the earth.

REASONS FOR POLLUTION

Because the relative impact of environmental disruption is a difficult thing to measure, it is somewhat meaningless to say that the Russians are more affected than we are, or vice versa. But what should be of interest is an attempt to ascertain why it is that pollution exists in a state-owned, centrally planned economy like that of the Soviet Union. Despite the fact that our economies differ, many if not all of the usual economic explanations for pollution in the non-communist world also hold for the Soviet Union. The Russians, too, have been unable to adjust their accounting system so that each enterprise pays not only its direct costs of production for labor, raw materials, and equipment but also its social costs of production arising from such by-products as dirty air and water. If the factory were charged for these social costs and had to take them into account when trying to make a profit on its operations, presumably factories would throw off less waste and would reuse or recycle their air and water. However, the precise social cost of such waste is difficult to measure and allocate under the best of circumstances, be it in the United States or the U.S.S.R. (In the Ruhr Valley in Germany, industries and municipalities are charged for the water they consume and discharge, but their system has shortcomings.)

In addition, almost everyone in the world regards air and water as free goods. Thus, even if it were always technologically feasible, it would still be awkward ideologically to charge for something that "belongs to everyone," particularly in a communist society. For a variety of reasons, therefore, air and water in the U.S.S.R. are treated as free or undervalued goods. When anything is free, there is a tendency to consume it without regard for future consequences. But with water and air, as with free love, there is a limit to the amount available to be consumed, and after a time there is the risk of exhaustion. We saw an illustration of this principle in the use of water for irrigation. Since water was treated virtually as a free good, the Russians did not care how much water they lost through unlined canals or how much water they used to irrigate the soil.

Similarly, the Russians have not been able to create clear lines of authority and responsibility for enforcing pollution-control regulations. As in the United States, various Russian agencies, from the Ministry of Agriculture to the Ministry of Public Health, have some but not ultimate say in coping with the problem. Frequently when an agency does attempt to enforce a law, the polluter will deliberately choose to break the law. As we saw at Lake Baikal, this is especially tempting when the penalty for breaking the law is only $55 a time, while the cost of eliminating the effluent may be in the millions of dollars.

The Russians also have to contend with an increase in population growth and the concentration of much of this increase in urban areas. In addition, this larger population has been the beneficiary of an increase in the quantity and complexity of production that accompanies industrialization. As a result, not only is each individual in the Soviet Union, as in the United States, provided with more goods to consume, but the resulting products, such as plastics and detergents, are more exotic and less easily disposed of than goods of an earlier, less complicated age.

Like their fellow inhabitants of the world, the Russians have to contend with something even more ominous than the Malthusian Principle. Malthus observed that the population increased at a geometric rate but that food production grew at only an arithmetic rate. If he really wants to be dismal, the economist of today has more to worry about. It is true that the population seems to be increasing at accelerated rates, but, whereas food production at least continues to increase, our air, water, and soil supplies are relatively constant. They can be renewed, just as crops can be replanted, but, for the most part, they cannot be expanded. In the long run, this "Doomsday Principle" may prove to be of more consequence than the Malthusian doctrine. With time and pollution we may simply run out of fresh air and water. Then, if the damage is not irreversible, a portion of the population will be eliminated and those who remain will exist until there is a shortage once again or until the air, water, and soil are irretrievably poisoned.

INCENTIVES TO POLLUTE UNDER SOCIALISM

In addition to the factors which confront all the people of the earth, regardless of their social or economic system, there are some reasons for polluting which seem to be peculiar to a socialist country such as the Soviet Union in its present state of economic development. First of all, state officials in the Soviet Union are judged almost entirely by how much they are able to increase their region's economic growth. Thus, government officials are not likely to be promoted if they decide to act as impartial referees between contending factions on questions of pollution. State officials identify with the polluters, not the conservationists, because the polluters will increase economic growth and the prosperity of the region while the antipolluters want to divert resources away from increased production. There is almost a political as well as an economic imperative to devour idle resources. The limnologists at Lake Baikal fear no one so much as the voracious Gosplan (State Planning) officials and their allies in the regional government offices. These officials do not have to face a voting constituency which might reflect the conservation point of view, such as the League of Women Voters or the Sierra Club in this country. It is true that there are outspoken conservationists in the U.S.S.R. who are often supported by the Soviet press, but for the most part they do not have a vote. Thus the lime smelters continued to smoke away behind the resort area of Kislovodsk even though critics in *Izvestiia, Literaturnaya Gazeta, Sovetskaia Rossiia, Trud,* and *Krokodil* protested long and loud.

At one time state governments in our country often reflected similar onesidedness. Maine, for example, was often cited as an area where industry did what it wanted to do to nature. Now, as the conservationist voting bloc has grown in size, the Maine state government finds itself acting as referee. Accordingly it has passed a far-reaching law which regulates the location and operation of all new industry. Failure to have voted for such legislation may have meant defeat at the polls for many politicians. No such device for transmitting voting pressure exists at present in the U.S.S.R.

Second, industrialization has come relatively recently to the U.S.S.R. and so the Russians continue to emphasize the increase in production. Pollution control generally appears to be nonproductive, and there is usually resistance to the diversion of resources from productive to nonproductive purposes. This is even reflected in the words used to describe the various choices. "Conserve" generally seems to stand in opposition to "produce."

Third, until July 1967, all raw materials in the ground were treated by the Russians as free goods. As a result, whenever the mine operator or oil driller had exploited the most accessible oil and ore, he moved on to a new site where the average variable costs were lower. This has resulted in very low recovery rates and the discarding of large quantities of salvageable materials, which increase the amount of waste to be disposed of.

Fourth, as we have seen, it is as hard for the Russians as it is for us to include social costs in factory-pricing calculations. However, not only do they have to worry about social cost accounting, they also are unable to reflect all the private cost considerations. Because there is no private ownership of land, there are no private property owners to protest the abuse of various resources. Occasionally it does happen that a private property owner in the United States calculates that his private benefits from selling his land for use in some new disruptive use is *not* greater than the private cost he would bear as a result of not being able to use the land any more. So he retains the land as it is. The lack of such private property holders or resort owners and of such a calculation seems to be the major reason why erosion is destroying the Black Sea coast. There is no one who can lay claim to the pebbles on the shore front, and so they are free to anyone who wants to cart them away. Of course private landowners do often decide to sell their land, especially if the new use is to be for oil exploitation rather than pebble exploitation. Then the private benefits to the former owner are high and the social costs are ignored, as always. The Russians, however, under their existing system, now only have to worry about accounting for social costs, they lack the first line of protection that would come from balancing private costs and private benefits.

Fifth, economic growth in the U.S.S.R. has been even more unbalanced, and in some cases more onesided, than in the United States. Thus, occasionally change takes place so rapidly and on such a massive scale in a state-run economy that there is no time to reflect on all the consequences. In the early 1960's, Khrushchev decided that the Soviet Union needed a large chemical industry. All at once chemical plants began to spring up or expand all over the country. In their anxiety to fulfill their targets for new plant construction, few if any of the planners were able to devote much attention to the disruptive effects on the environment that such plants might have. We saw one result at Yasnaya Polyana. In fact, the power of the state to make fundamental changes may be so great that irreversible changes may frequently be inflicted on the environment without anyone's realizing what is happening until it is too late. This seems to be the best explanation of the meteorological disruption that is taking place in Siberia. It is easier for an allpowerful organism like the state than for a group of private entrepreneurs to build the reservoirs and reverse the rivers. Private enterprises can cause their own havoc, as our own dust bowl experience or our use of certain pesticides or sedatives indicates, but in the absence of private business or property interests the state's powers can be much more far-reaching in scope. In an age of rampant technology, where the consequences of one's actions are not always fully anticipated, even well-intentioned programs can have disastrous effects on the environmental status quo.

ADVANTAGES OF A SOCIALIST SYSTEM

Amidst all these problems, there are some things the Russians do very well. For example, the Russians have the power to prevent the production of various products. Thus, the Soviet Union is the only country in the world that does not put ethyl lead in most of the gasoline it produces. This may be due to technical lag as much as to considerations of health, but the result is considerably more lead-free gasoline. Similarly, the Russians have not permitted as much emphasis on consumer-goods production as we have in the West. Consequently there is less waste to discard. Russian consumers may be somewhat less enthusiastic about this than the ecologists and conservationists, but in the U.S.S.R. there are no disposable bottles or disposable diapers to worry about. It also happens that, because labor costs are low relative to the price of goods, more emphasis is placed on prolonging the life of various products. In other words it is worthwhile to use labor to pick up bottles and collect junk. No one would intentionally abandon his car on a Moscow street, as 50,000 people did in New York City in 1969. Even if a Russian car is 20 years old, it is still valuable. Because of the price relationships that exist in the U.S.S.R., the junkman can still make a profit. This facilitates the recycling process, which ecologists tell us is the ultimate solution to environmental disruption.

It should also be remembered that, while not all Russian laws are observed, the Russians do have an effective law enforcement system which they have periodically brought to bear in the past. Similarly, they have the power to set aside land for use as natural preserves. The lack of private land ownership makes this a much easier process to implement than in the United States. As of 1969, the Soviet Government had set aside 80 such preserves, encompassing nearly 65,000 square kilometers.

Again because they own all the utilities as well as most of the buildings, the Russians have stressed the installation of centrally supplied steam. Thus, heating and hot water are provided by central stations, and this makes possible more efficient combustion and better smoke control than would be achieved if each building were to provide heat and hot water for itself. Although some American cities have similar systems, this approach is something we should know more about.

In sum, if the study of environmental disruption in the Soviet Union demonstrates anything, it shows that not private enterprise but industrialization is the primary cause of environmental disruption. This suggests that state ownership of all the productive resources is not a cure-all. The replacement of private greed by public greed is not much of an improvement. Currently the proposals for the solution of environmental disruption seem to be no more advanced in the U.S.S.R. than they are in the United States. One thing does seem clear, however, and that is that, unless the Russians change their ways, there seems little reason to believe that a strong centralized and planned economy has any notable advantages over other economic systems in solving environmental disruption.

REFERENCES AND NOTES

1. *Rabochaia Gaz.* 1967, 4 (15 Dec. 1967).
2. *Ekon. Gaz.* 1967, No. 4 37 (1967).
3. *Sovet. Moldaviia* 1969, 2 (1 June 1969).
4. V. G. Kriazhev, *Vnerabochee Vremia i Sphera Obslyzhivaniia* (Ekonomika, Moscow, 1966), p. 130.
5. *Soviet News* 1970, 6 (7 Apr. 1970).
6. *Turkm. Iskra* 1969, 3 (16 Sept. 1969).
7. O. Volkov, *Soviet Life* 1966, 6 (Aug. 1966).
8. L. Rossolimo, *Baikal* (Nauka, Moscow, 1966), p. 91.
9. I. Petrov, *Kommunist* 1969, No. 11, 74 (1969).
10. *Rabochaia Gaz.* 1969, 4 (27 June 1969); *Ekon. Gaz.* 1968, No. 4, 40 (1968); *Lit. Gaz.* 1967, No. 32, 10 (1967).
11. *Izv.* 1966, 5 (3 July 1966).
12. *Soviet News* 1969, 105 (11 March 1969).
13. I thank Leonard Kirsch of the University of Massachusetts, Boston, for his many suggestions, Elena Vorobey of the Library of the Russian Research Center for her valuable bibliographical help, and Wellesley College for its financial support.

Key Elements: Population and Energy

WHAT ETHICAL DILEMMAS UNDERLIE THE BASIC ENVIRONMENTAL PROBLEMS OF POPULATION AND ENERGY?

To what extent is society justified in imposing a limit on human procreation?

In developing an effective and humane population policy, what should be the role of voluntary versus coercive restraints?

In, what ways has the use of energy influenced the evolution of the modern world and man's modification of the natural environment?

Why must new sources of energy now be developed?

Assuming that you have a normal pulse beat, it will not quite keep up with the increase in world population. . . Every time your pulse throbs, the population of the world will have added more than one human being.

William Vogt

. . . exponential curves grow to infinity only in mathematics. In the physical world they either turn round and saturate, or they break down catastrophically. It is our duty as thinking men to do our best toward a gentle saturation, instead of sustaining the exponential growth, though this faces us with very unfamiliar and distasteful problems.

Dennis Gabor

The issue is, indeed, a religious one in the sense that it raises the question, 'What is the true end of man? Is it to populate the Earth with the maximum number of human beings or is it to enable human beings to lead the best kind of life. . . ?'

Arnold Toynbee

Population and the
Dignity of Man
Roger L. Shinn

At this stage of human history and knowledge, I need not waste time arguing that overpopulation is a threat to mankind. Human life is a glorious gift, but there can be too many lives for the good of man. The population explosion is the name we give to the multiplication of people at a rate that doubles the earth's population in approximately 35 years. We are familiar with the projections: if the present rate should continue, earth's 3.6 billion people in 1970 will be 7.2 billion by about 2005, 14.4 billion by about 2040, 28.2 billion by about 2075, and so on. We have heard that 600 years of such increase will mean a person for every square yard of earth (including arctic tundras, deserts and mountaintops), that after a little longer there will be a person for every square foot, that some day man will outweigh the earth, then the solar system, and even the universe. Obviously all this cannot happen, but nobody knows what amount of starvation, pestilence or carnage it will take to stop it. Humane methods of meeting the threat are possible, but nobody yet knows whether they are probable.

The problem arises because man is a unique being within nature, a creature who in some ways transcends nature and exercises a measure of control over nature. The powers in which he has often exulted now threaten him. He wonders whether he will outlive the rats and roaches, or whether the abilities that have enabled him in some ways to outwit nature now doom him. Loren Eiseley has said it with characteristic eloquence:

> It is with the coming of man that a vast hole seems to open in nature, a vast black whirlpool spinning faster and faster, consuming flesh, stones, soil, minerals, sucking down the lightning, wrenching power from the atom, until the ancient sounds of nature are drowned in the cacophony of something which is no longer nature, something instead which is loose and knocking at the world's heart, something demonic and no longer planned—escaped, it may be—spewed out of nature, contending in a final giant's game against its master. [*The Firmament of Time* (Atheneum, 1962, p. 123).]

Thus an anthropologist puts in contemporary language an ancient biblical theme—that man's creativity is intimately related to his destructiveness. In the language of theological tradition, mankind, although not conspicuously obedient to most of the divine commands, has prodigiously carried out the first of them: "Be fruitful and multiply, and fill the earth and subdue it" (Gen. 1:28). If Immanuel Kant, bachelor and moral philosopher, were present, he would immediately point out that even if man in this case did what was commanded, he did not do so *because* it was commanded. He had his own reasons, and he was the victim of unreckoned facts and unreasoned desires. Granted. But the consequence of radical conformity to this one command or invitation and neglect of others is the population crisis.

The population explosion is a moral problem. Like most moral problems in modern civilization, it has important scientific and technological aspects. But it is a moral issue because it involves questions of the good of man, of values and conflicts of values, of man's self-esteem in relation to the rest of creation, of relations between personal, tribal or national purposes and the welfare of the human race.

Hence we may wonder why theology and the church have not spoken and acted more emphatically on this issue. There has been no lack of bold statements on other intense controversies of our time. I do not argue that the church at large is an immensely radical force in the contemporary world. But its centers of leadership and intellectual energy have not hesitated to affront the public mood with strong stands on questions of race, economic justice, revolution. They have been more timid, even inhibited, on the question of population.

In 1960 Richard M. Fagley of the Commission of the Churches on International Affairs (an organ of the World Council of Churches) produced a good book, *The Population Explosion and Christian Responsibility* (Oxford University Press). The Geneva Conference on Church and Society, convened by the World Council of Churches in 1966, said some sensible things about the necessity for restraining population growth, as did the Fourth Assembly of the World Council of Churches at Uppsala in 1968. But the debates and the findings were marked by a caution uncharacteristic of those bodies on some other controversial issues. The Board of Christian Social Concerns of the United Methodist Church is exceptional in urging recognition that "families with more than two children contribute to the population explosion."

There are reasons for the reluctance of the church to mount crusades on this issue. To determine whether the reasons are valid requires an analysis in some detail.

CAUGHT BY SURPRISE

One reason for the perplexity of the modern church and of modern man over population problems is the way in which the human race has been caught by surprise. Population pressures on a world scale are recent. Regionally they are an old problem, often met in the past by exposure of infants, abandonment of the aged and conquest of the lands of others—all methods that raise severe ethical questions. But the question of an overpopulated *world* is not one on which traditional wisdom has spent much energy.

Prophecy is not the same as prediction, and the prophets of Christianity and the world religions did not predict the present situation. The demographers were not much better. The records of the 1930s abound in dire predictions of depopulation due to the reluctance of many families to reproduce their own numbers.

In one sense the population explosion came with incredible speed. It took all of human history until 1850—some say a million years, others say far longer—for Earth's population to rise to a billion persons; now we add a billion in less than 15 years. This is not simply acceleration; it is transformation. It requires major reconsideration of ethical traditions, prestige symbols, political practices, family mores.

But in another sense the rapid change slipped up on us. It was not marked by any instantaneous event—like the destruction of Hiroshima or the 1969 Hurricane Camille—that alerted governments to instantaneous action. In a way everything happened gradually. There was a lag between certain acts and their consequences: at a minimum the familiar nine-month lag, on the big scale a much longer lag, between many personal acts and their momentous social consequences. Because immense change was never immediately discernible, men always found more urgent problems to work on. People might get concerned about projections of future crisis, but there was no shortage of immediate crises demanding response; so the population problem was filed in the back of many minds as an issue to get around to some day.

Yet all the time the future emergency was becoming visible in present emergencies, and rather suddenly in the past decade a large part of the world realized that disaster is imminent. Anthony Lewis recently reported in the *New York Times* (December 15, 1969) the fairly widespread view among scientists that the human race has 35 to 100 years of life left on earth, with population the biggest single element in the threatening syndrome. Scientists John Platt writes about "a shorter life expectancy than people have ever had in the world before," and he estimates, "We may have even less than a 50-50 chance of living until 1980" (*Science*, November 28, 1969, p. 1116). If nuclear weapons pose the most immediate threat, in his judgment population is not far behind. Paul Ehrlich predicts that even the most effective crash programs can no longer prevent starvation of hundreds of millions of people in the 1970s (*The Population Bomb* [Ballantine Books, 1968], Prologue). And if—as certain authorities think—the agricultural revolution refutes his predictions, the fact remains that it only delays the disaster unless mankind does something to limit its numbers. Meanwhile, if the world should manage to feed people more successfully than it is now doing, its educational, social and political institutions seem unable to cope with exploding populations.

Such a situation calls for revision of inherited values and ethical criteria. Part of the work of ethics is always to shake loose from old ethical modes. Ethics is the worst enemy of ethics—traditional ethics or innovative ethics. Yet an innovative ethic can rarely simply scorn and destroy the ethic it would replace, because the tradition may have something precious in it. The traditional ethic embodies a concern for human life—including helpless life of infants, life still in the womb, even potential human life. That ethic may make us wince when we hear callous talk of surplus people, as though not every person were valuable. We cannot demolish that ethic without destroying something of our humanity. The question is how the concern for life that created the ethic may today require its revision. Such decisions are made not by a few professional intellectuals, but by the intricate processes and symbol-systems of whole societies. Modern man and the modern church, caught by surprise, are engaged in that process of revision. It takes time—but not much time is available.

DOCTRINAL INHIBITIONS

Ethical transformation, which is always precarious, becomes particularly difficult in this case because it is compounded by some specific religious and doctrinal inhibitions that have influenced men's perception of the problem. The Christianity that has contributed to the concern for persons in our ethical heritage has also frequently harbored within itself docetic and Manichean heresies that demeaned the flesh. One expression of this mood has been the exaltation of celibacy, which if it were persuasive to enough people might solve the population problem. More common has been a grudging acceptance of sexual activity as a necessary part of procreation and as ethically justifiable only when procreation was intended. The result is the anticontraceptive mentality that persists in some Christian thinking to this day.

I describe this attitude as heretical because it is contrary to the joyful biblical celebration of the flesh, marked by the words of Genesis that are later quoted by Jesus: "Therefore a man leaves his father and his mother and cleaves to his wife, and they become one flesh" (Gen. 2:24, Mark 10:7). The issue here is a subtle one. There are forms of heroic service, involving renunciation of many of life's delights, that are in no sense heretical. But the docetic contempt for the flesh, frequently denounced as heretical, kept creeping back into Christianity and sometimes permeated its cultural expressions.

Today Christianity is working its way out of that bind. The issue is one of several in which the pressures of the secular world are helping the church to rediscover its own biblical heritage. But the process moves at an uneven pace. Within Roman Catholicism most theologians of the United States and northern Europe are ready to advocate contraceptives, both because of the demographic problem and because of the meaning of the sexual relationship within marriage. They regret that the papacy, counteracting a 70-14 vote of the Papal Commission on Birth Control, remains on record as opposed to contraception. Catholic laymen in many areas have resolved the problem with their own consciences, often with outspoken support from priests. In any event, considerable evidence shows that Catholic families, on a worldwide basis, are not distinguished by large size.

Eastern Orthodoxy has no centralized teaching authority comparable to the papacy, and it looks for guidance less to dogma than to a mystical sense of tradition, which is not precisely formulated and which is subject to development. Thus far the tradition is largely anticontraceptive. Although there are elements of the tradition that make change on this issue foreseeable, the Orthodox churches are largely silent on the question of population.

By and large, Protestantism has accepted contraceptives and the importance of limiting family size, whether out of authentic theological insight (as I would like to believe) or out of easy adaptation to the spirit of the times (as some critics would charge). All the major Protestant denominations in the United States and the predominantly Protestant National Council of Churches have adopted statements endorsing family planning.

The caution of the World Council of Churches (mentioned above) is not due to a lingering docetic heresy. It can be attributed to a reluctance of Protestant leaders to offend groups (the Eastern Orthodox within the council and Roman Catholics outside it) with whom they are just beginning to learn to live in peace.

AN IDEOLOGICAL STRUGGLE

In most international discussions of population and economic development, an ideological argument frequently skews the considerations. The advocacy of population control is taken to be the ideology of affluent whites, and it may be rejected by spokesmen for Asia, Latin America and Africa. Likewise within the United States there is increasing resentment in the black ghettos toward organizations, usually white dominated, that advocate family planning. The economically deprived, who are often also the dark-skinned, resent the exhortations (as they hear them) of affluent whites advising them to limit their population. They may respond by rhetorical resistance to ethnic suicide or genocide.

They have a point. That is, impoverished peoples have a right to resist the advice of wealthy peoples, who use the population problem as an evasion of their moral responsibility to the poor whom they have exploited. Racial and economic exploitation are conspicuous facts in our world. And there is plenty of evidence that programs of economic aid to underdeveloped nations and groups are *(1)* pitifully inadequate in scope and *(2)* often cunningly contrived to help donors more than recipients. When affluent societies then righteously complain of their sacrifices and blame the poor for breeding habits that keep them poor, anger is an appropriate response.

This ideological issue is another reason why the World Council of Churches has been cautious on the population problem. In its deliberations the issue is usually raised by white Westerners within the context of discussions about economic development. The answer usually comes from Asians or Latin Americans who tell the spokesmen from more industrialized societies that they cannot use this device to evade their responsibilities.

Archbishop Helder Camara, a courageous champion of the poor in Brazil, has made the point well in objecting to the "smokescreens" that have obscured international economic problems. Writing in *The Christian Century* for December 10, 1969, he says: "One such smokescreen is the insistence that the Third World's problems would be eased if a massive birth control program—that modern cure-all—were to be imposed on that world." Let us clearly grant three valid points in that sentence: *(1)* birth control is no cure-all; *(2)* it will not resolve the economic problems of Latin America or any other area; and *(3)* it cannot be "imposed" on any society without destructive consequences.

The other side of the story is that no other solutions will do much for Latin America, Africa or Asia unless these societies check their eruption in population. To this extent Malthus remains unanswered and unanswerable: no social devices, however ingenious, can counter the inexorable logic of the geometric progression. Interestingly, Marxism has recognized the issue. Marxists at times have indulged in gibberish to the effect that overpopulation was a bogey of capitalist societies with their deliberate restraint of production; but lately most Marxist societies have seen the importance of policies to restrain population expansion.

One important fact remains to deideologize the discussion. The limitation of population is as urgent a demand upon the wealthiest societies today as upon the poorest. The affluent have no right to ask the poor to adopt a discipline that their condescending advisers reject. If starvation is a more urgent problem for India than for the United States, the ecological destruction wrought by an expanding high-consuming United States is greater than that inflicted by the "teeming populations" of Asia.

The United States, whose 6 per cent of the world's population consumes something like 40 per cent of the world's production, manages to despoil its own homeland and exploit the homelands of others. Its combination of rising population and rising standard of living congests its natural areas and produces emergencies of waste disposal in most of its cities. John Platt says (in the article mentioned above) that "many scientists fear the destruction of our whole biological and ecological balance" within the next 20 years.

Man knows too little of ecology to reckon accurately the risks he is taking. But a few examples are clues to the danger. Industrial man fills the air with carbon dioxide from combustion, while he reduces oxygen-producing plants and forests. He does not know at what point the upset of atmospheric balance may create disaster, perhaps increasing the earth's temperature and melting polar ice caps, thus raising ocean levels and inundating coastal cities and plains. Again, the increased use of chemical fertilizers pours phosphates and nitrates into streams and lakes, spurring the growth of algae, while the discharge of sewage magnifies the same effects, thus fouling clear waterways and destroying fresh-water fish.

Over Kennedy airport alone airliners in a year discharge 10,000 tons of carbon monoxide, 3,000 tons of hydrocarbons, 330 tons of nitrogen oxides, and 100 tons of particulates, largely carbons. I am ready to guess that the scientists coming to the annual meeting of the American Association for the Advancement of Science pour more poisons into the atmosphere by this one trip than they would emit in a lifetime if they were desperately poor villagers in India. And probably they consume more paper in these few days than they would in a peasant lifetime almost anywhere in Asia.

The answer is not solely population control. What is needed is a technology directed more toward a profit-and-loss statement for the total society and its environment, less to the balance sheets of competing corporations. Even so, the overwhelming probability is that this world cannot endure simultaneously rising numbers of people and rising standards of living. Population is not the problem solely of the poorer classes and societies; it is even more urgently the problem of the affluent.

WESTERN CHRISTIANITY'S PREDATORY LEGACY

The issues of ecology require an inquiry into the cultural and theological history of those civilizations that have done most to plunder the earth. François Mergen, dean of Yale's school of forestry, has said, "Sometimes I think the students who earn degrees in ecology should be ordained—they're so serious." Beyond his witticism one detects a curious relation-ship between theology and ecological dilemmas.

Cultural historians have frequently pointed to a relation-ship between biblical faith and technological progress. Perhaps it is not sheer accident that technology has developed in civilizations influenced by the Hebrew-Christian Scriptures. The Bible in its radical monotheism desacralizes nature. Sun, moon and stars are no longer divine and they may not be worshipped. Brooks and trees are no longer inhabited by spirits. There is one God; the world is his creation. Man, given dominion, may investigate and appropriate the objects of nature. No taboos, no forbidding mysteries, no divinities block enterprising man. In recent years theologians like Harvey Cox and Arend van Leeuwen have taken up this theme in hymns of praise to urban, technological civilization.

But historian Lynn White has investigated this same theme with a chastened conscience. In his 1966 address to the Washington meeting of the American Association for the Advancement of Science, he told Christians, in effect: repent, don't boast over this technological prowess. Within three years the ripple effect of this address has reached far into literature and journalism about technology and ecology. In White's words, "The victory of Christianity over paganism was the greatest psychic revolution in the history of our culture," and its effects persist in this era often called a post-Christian age. "Especially in its Western form," says White, "Christianity is the most anthropocentric religion the world has seen. . . . By destroying pagan animism, Christianity made it possible to exploit nature in a mood of indifference to the feelings of natural objects." Tracing the story of the union, little more than a century ago, of the previously diverse histories of science and of technology, he finds that they "joined to give mankind powers which, to judge by many of the ecologic effects, are out of control." And for this history, he maintains, "Christianity bears a huge burden of guilt" (*Science*, March 10, 1967, p. 1205).

Other scholars from other disciplines have been making comparable inquiries. Economists Barbara Ward and Kenneth Boulding have made familiar the symbol of the earth as a spaceship. This planet earth, says Miss Ward, "has acquired the intimacy, the fellowship, and the vulnerability of a spaceship" (*Spaceship Earth* [Columbia University Press, 1966], p. v). Boulding puts it:

> We have to visualize the earth as a small, rather crowded spaceship, destination unknown, in which man has to find a slender thread of a way of life in the midst of a continually repeatable cycle of material transformations. In a spaceship, there can be no inputs or outputs. . . . Up to now the human population has been small enough so that we have not had to regard the earth as a spaceship. We have been able to regard the atmosphere and the oceans and even the soil as an inexhaustible reservoir, from which we can draw at will and which we can pollute at will. There is writing on the wall, however. . . . As the spaceship society approaches, therefore, we must move towards an extremely conservationist point of view, in which every scrap of material substratum of human environment and culture is carefully scrutinized, identified, and followed through a cycle which is capable of being sustained indefinitely. ["The Wisdom of Man and the Wisdom of God," *Human Values on Spaceship Earth* (National Council of Churches, 1966), pp. 6, 8.]

Boulding is a Quaker Christian, and he thinks the new society may call for a closer adherence to the ethic of Jesus than recent centuries gave it. But he finds profoundly inadequate the inherited form of the Christian ethic and suggests that in an ecumenical age we may need to learn from the ethic of the East: "The East has never had any illusions about being able to conquer nature, and has always regarded man as living in a somewhat precarious position, as a guest of doubtful welcome, shall we say, in the great household of the natural world" *(ibid.).*

Lynn White, also a Christian, sees a wisdom in Zen Buddhism that *is* appropriate to our needs. But he proposes also that the radical Christianity of St. Francis of Assisi may inform us that we men live in this world with birds and wolves, with Brother Ant and Sister Fire, who praise "the Creator in their own ways as Brother Man does in his" (*op. cit.*).

We often hear that the technology that has, in a sense, made our ecological problems is the power that can answer them. But if this technology is basically predatory in spirit and is allied with a predatory religious spirit, the fact may be that some reformation of technological and religious spirit is required in our time. Such is the judgment of William Pollard, nuclear physicist and theologian:

> One hears much these days, and gratefully so, about conservation of natural resources, environmental health, pollution control, beautification programs, wilderness and wildlife preservation. This is of course all very necessary. But almost completely lacking from all such discussion is a sense of the sacredness and holiness of the earth, or of the awful dimension of the sacrilege which man has wrought in spoiling it. What is needed at this juncture more than anything else is a theology of nature. ["Toward a Theology of Nature," unpublished paper prepared for the Joint Commission on the Church in Human Affairs, August 1968, p. 9.]

White's conclusion is similar: "Both our present science and our present technology are so tinctured with orthodox Christian arrogance toward nature that no solution for our ecologic crisis can be expected from them alone. Since the roots of our trouble are so largely religious, the remedy must also be essentially religious, whether we call it that or not. We must rethink and refeel our nature and destiny" (*op. cit.*).

If there is any truth in the observations of Boulding, Pollard and White—as I believe there is—man cannot meet his population problem solely by more effective contraceptive technology and by marshaling the technology of persuasion to convince masses of people to abide by the ethic of the new high priests of demography and ecology.

Modern man must revise his sense of his own relationship to nature and to his fellow men.

FREEDOM, COERCION AND RESPONSIBILITY

Man's relation to nature and to his fellow men bears upon the most difficult ethical problem connected with population: the problem of human freedom. To what extent is society justified in limiting the right of persons to procreate? This right is usually considered a basic personal right; yet society suffers when persons exercise the right irresponsibly.

One conference called by the World Council of Churches walked directly into the dilemma without finding the way out. At the Geneva Conference on Church and Society, Section IV on Man and Community in Changing Societies came to these two different findings:

> Responsible parenthood is not just a matter of individual family concern: it must be accepted as an integral part of the social ethic of the day. (Par. 60.)
>
> Every couple has a right to make its own responsible decisions on the planning of its own family in accord with its moral and religious convictions. (Par. 105.) [Official Report (World Council of Churches, 1967), pp. 167, 178.]

The earlier paragraph points out that procreation is a social issue requiring an ethic that reaches beyond individual families; the latter paragraph reverts to the more traditional location of the issue within the family. Anyone familiar with the drafting methods of assemblies seeking consensus can guess that the two paragraphs came from two subcommittees with diverging opinions and that the larger group never succeeded in reconciling the differences. (Note, however, that this conference was not an assembly of the W.C.C. and did not speak for the council.)

The United Nations often struggles with similar dilemmas. The Universal Declaration of Human Rights, adopted by the

General Assembly on December 1, 1948, declared: "men and women of full age, without any limitation due to race, nationality or religion, have the right to marry and to found a family" (Article 16).

By December of 1966 the General Assembly, while still giving "due regard to the principle that the size of the family should be the free choice of each individual family," expressed clearly its concern for the "economic, social, cultural, psychological and health factors" in demography. And U Thant, the secretary-general, said: "Economic development at the level necessary to improve the quality of individual life demands also that the scale of human reproduction be moderated according to each family's deliberate desires, its religious convictions and its ability to provide."

In the nature of the case the General Assembly and the secretary-general must do all they can to minimize any possible conflict between the emphasis on freedom of the family and the social perils that may result from that freedom. Others are not so constrained. A long-nascent conflict of values among those concerned about population is suddenly erupting as an obvious controversy. The past emphasis has been upon freedom of the family to determine its own size, independent from external controls, ecclesiastical or political. The newly voiced emphasis is upon the necessity for measures to require families to limit reproduction.

The conflict was vividly illustrated in two successive issues of the *New York Times.* On September 21, 1969, a dispatch by Harold M. Schmeck, Jr., was headlined: "Family Planning: New Focus in U.S." It reported that the federal administration was giving high priority to "the related issues of population and family planning," with reliance upon the desire of many people to space their children if only they had access to information and methods. On September 22 the headline of a dispatch filed by Gladwin Hill read: "Scientists Tell Nixon Adviser Voluntary Birth Control Is 'Insanity.' " The text told of a meeting in Aspen, Colorado, where Garrett

Hardin, spokesman for a group of specialists, said to presidential counsel John Erlichman: "In the long run, voluntarism is insanity. The result will be continued uncontrolled population growth."

At this stage in human history there is considerable agreement among those most knowledgeable and most concerned about population that a zero growth rate for the human race has become desirable. There is equal agreement that purely voluntary methods, even assuming vastly increased education and distribution of contraceptives, will not quickly bring the zero rate. Hence it is not surprising that some persons, deeply concerned about the issue, are raising questions about the necessity for compulsion. Paul Ehrlich wonders why society readily practices the coercion of war, yet shudders at coercion in constraint of reproduction (*op. cit.*, p. 166). Kenneth Boulding, a social scientist as sensitive to human values as any, has proposed an ingenious plan for combining government regulation and personal freedom to achieve the zero growth rate (*The Meaning of the Twentieth Century* [Harper & Row, 1964], Ch. 6, "The Population Trap"). Bernard Berelson, president of the Population Council, has catalogued an immense variety of plans for limitation, ranging from coercive to voluntary (*Science*, February 7, 1969, pp. 533-43).

Conflicts of values, usually painful conflicts, are part of almost all serious ethical decision. So it is with population policy. A desperate world may use coercion to limit population, as single societies have sometimes done in the past. But the dilemma is a bitter one. We started with a concern for the dignity of man. Human dignity demands limitation of population. But some methods of limitation destroy dignity. Infanticide, for example, is as bad as any problem it is designed to solve. It may remind us of the army officer who explained that he had to destroy a village in Vietnam in order to save it. Compulsory abortion or sterilization are a shade less brutal, but they so violate the consciences of many people as to be destructive of dignity.

In any crisis society qualifies personal rights, but part of ethical wisdom is to avoid crises that permit only destructive choices, and another part of wisdom is to maintain a maximum of human integrity even in crisis. Certainly any humane population policy will seek a maximum of free decision, a minimum of coercion. Hence it is encouraging to find Philip Hauser, director of the University of Chicago Population Research and Training Center, saying: "The fact is that decreases in fertility in what are now the economically advanced nations were achieved completely on a voluntary basis" (*Population Crisis*, Part 2, 1967-68 [U.S. Government Printing Office, 1968], p. 492). It is encouraging to hear Roger Revelle, director of the Harvard Center for Population Studies, call for an emphasis on "the drama of living human beings" rather than on quantitative calculations alone. Revelle points out that a social security system reduces the motivation for large families in those societies where parents must rely for old-age security on their sons, that a reduction in child mortality (while temporarily increasing population) reduces the incentive of parents to conceive many children (*Population Crisis*, Part 5-B, 1966 [U.S. Government Printing Office, 1967], pp. 1532-39). Such attention to wider cultural and ethical considerations relieves the starkness of the dilemma of destructive freedom and destructive coercion.

Yet mankind can never expect to evade the dilemma. Life permits no total freedom or total coercion. Society, if it is to survive, will probably learn to limit population by means of persuasion and pressure that fall somewhere between uninhibited freedom and overt coercion. Many methods of persuasion and pressure are possible. Prestige systems, economic pressures, taxation, housing policies and skillfully contrived propaganda are a few of the devices by which societies are likely to move increasingly as they see the necessity of limiting reproduction. It is not wrong for society to use such pressures. Society itself is under immense pressure; there is no reason why the families within it should evade the pressures.

Yet there is danger in the propensity of society to manipulate its members for their own good. Donald Michael has pointed to one of the basic conflicts of our time: man increasingly sees himself as a manipulable and manipulated object among other objects in social and physical systems; yet he increasingly rebels with humanistic passion against this premise that he is a manipulable object. In the few years since Donald Michael published those reflections (*The Next Generation* [Vintage Books, 1965], pp. 163-65) a generation of college students has made its protests so loud that society cannot block out the noise. Participatory democracy is rarely tidy and is not always wise; yet it has *élan*. Population policies that emerge from participatory democracy, informed by accurate knowledge, can accomplish some results unattainable by methods that impose elitist solutions on unwilling people.

Yet there is much that is still unknown about the ways of relating personal freedom and social responsibility in this technological age. Any theological and humanistic ethic must ponder such questions deeply. Their answer will have much to say for our beliefs concerning the identity and dignity of man.

All those who have studied the past from the standpoint of economics, and those especially who have studied economic geography, are aware that from the material point of view, history is primarily the story of the increasing ability of man to reach and control energy.

Energy and Man: A Symposium

. . . . . . The transformation of energy for human use, which has been primarily an engineering and technological problem in the past, will increasingly become an economic, political and moral problem in the next thirty years.

Kaiser News

The Energy
Revolution:
Peril and Promise
George Taylor

The energy revolution has transformed America. One has only to contrast the society of Washington and Jefferson with that of the 1960s. Energy has been developed in such varieties and in such abundance that it has changed the daily life of every person. It has at times been more decisive than ideologies and it has often left economic and social institutions obsolete as man has continued an apparent conquest of his physical environment.

The change has been dramatic. A century ago, the muscle power of men and domestic animals supplied 94 percent of the world's energy needs; fossil fuels like coal and oil supplied only 5 percent. Today the situation is reversed. The industrialized nations now obtain 93 percent of their energy needs from coal, oil and natural gas; the muscle power of men and animals provides only 6 percent and waterpower contributes 1 percent.

In the past half century, the burdens of darkness, discomfort and drudgery have been replaced by light and heat and comfort. Candles have given way to electric lights and wood fires for cooking have been replaced by gas and electricity. The plentiful supplies of energy in the home, on the farm and in the factory have created producing and consuming capacities beyond the dreams of utopians. Energy has laid the basis for transportation and communications which have made this nation the most mobile society in history.

The changes set loose by the energy revolution will doubtlessly accelerate. The U.S. population is expected to exceed 300 million by the year 2000. Thus there will be an increase as well in the current problems of promoting economic growth and achieving full employment, of raising living standards and maintaining a costly defense program, of protecting the environment, of exploring outer space and aiding the developing nations. The present stupendous demands on energy resources, raw materials and land and water shrink when compared to the soaring demands foreseen for the next four decades.

About five-sixths of all the fossil fuels—such as coal, oil and natural gas—consumed since the beginning of their use have taken place over the past 60 years. The total consumption of all such fuels used before the year 1900 would not last 5 years at today's rate of consumption.

The pressure of more and more people and their needs is the basic factor here and throughout the world in attempting to answer the inevitable question: Will there be enough to go around?

Here in the United States the immediate question is whether we have sufficient supplies of energy to sustain a rate of economic growth necessary to accomplish the essential goals of America's domestic and foreign policies.

One thing is sure. With all of man's ingenuity and adaptability and thirst for more and more knowledge, he still must work within the limitations imposed by the earth's natural environment.

Reverend Thomas Malthus of England postulated over 160 years ago that population growth tended to outstrip its means of subsistence. In his view and that of latter-day Malthusians, this built-in imbalance was periodically "corrected" by economic depressions, poverty, disease, pestilence and famine.

Malthus did not foresee the decline in the birthrate in industrial countries which has taken place. He did not foresee the growth of a new agricultural technology which has resulted in immense increases in per acre yield in spite of only a moderate increase in land under cultivation. Nor did he foresee the new sources of energy, together with increasingly efficient methods of discovery, extraction, processing, transportation and use. Science has released humanity from the despairing destiny implicit in Malthus' philosophy.

But there are warning signals. Most people in the world still go to bed hungry. Famines still sweep countries like China and India, with a major famine feared in India within the next decade.

In the United States itself there is a blind and optimistic reliance on the ability of science and technology to find all the answers to the problem of supplying enough energy, food, water and raw materials to meet the voracious demand of an increasing population and an expanding economy.

Often overlooked is the fact that the effect of the energy revolution is at variance with nature's scheme of conservation of raw materials and energy which had endured for millions of years before the impact of the late-comer, man, began to be felt.

And, too, the more the environment is modified by human beings, the more interdependent human institutions become and so the more easily they can be disrupted.

The history of the heedless exploitation of natural resources in building up this nation to its 20th century greatness is well known. Yet topsoil laboriously built up through centuries is still exposed by the bulldozer, the axe and power saw, or by the farmer, to be washed away by the rains or scattered by the winds. In many areas the water cycle has been destructively disrupted. Human and industrial wastes continue to befoul streams and rivers. Clean air is now being laden with contaminants from motor vehicles, industrial processes and coal-fired power plants. Poisonous radioactive fallout still drifts across continents as a result of previous testing of nuclear weapons in the atmosphere.

As biologist Dr. Barry Commoner said in a recent speech: ". . . the vast new powers of science carry with them equally vast and equally new responsibilities." Commoner urged that scientists, citizens and government administrators work together to "find the means to preserve . . . the water, the air and the soil and to conserve the resources of this planet for their proper service to the welfare of man."

It is imperative that the new energy revolution be for people. Unless it is guided by well-defined and progressive national economic and social policies and goals, together with all necessary social controls, the new age of energy abundance will not mean a more satisfactory life for most people nor can it meet their yet unfulfilled needs and aspirations.

TRENDS IN THE USE OF ENERGY

An epic story lies behind the cold statistics on the uses of energy in America. It is a story of how man found a nation richly endowed with coal, oil, natural gas and falling water and used these resources with vigor and ingenuity to transform an agricultural economy and build a mighty industrial civilization.

The enormous increases in the use of energy fuels have been stimulated in great part by a rising population, by shifts from older to newer fuels, by higher income and living levels. These changes have continuously increased per capita energy use. At the same time, there have been fewer and fewer workers involved in the extraction, processing and transportation of energy fuels in proportion to total economic activity.

Between 1900 and 1960 the use of energy for all purposes by Americans increased by 500 percent. In 1960, the United States consumed the energy equivalent of 8 million barrels of oil, nearly 2 million tons of coal and about 45 trillion cubic feet of natural gas.

In contrast to this five-fold increase in energy consumption over six decades the population of the U.S. rose by 142 percent and the per capita use of energy moved upward by almost 250 percent.

With only about 6 percent of the world's population, the United States uses one-third of the total world production of energy. It has an annual per capita rate of use six times that of the average per capita use of the rest of the world. Each American man, woman and child has working for him each year, either directly or indirectly, the equivalent of the energy contained in 9 tons of coal.

In 1850, the U.S. derived 90.6 percent of its energy (other than that supplied by the muscles of men and of domestic animals) from the burning of wood in industry, for heating and transportation purposes. The remaining 9.4 percent of the aggregate national energy consumption was obtained from the burning of bituminous and anthracite coal.

Fifty years later, by 1900, fuel wood had been superseded by coal as the principal energy source for the nation—70.3 percent coal, 20.7 percent fuel wood. By 1900, the second great shift in energy fuel sources was beginning—petroleum, natural gas and hydropower together were accounting for 9 percent of total U.S. energy use for all purposes.

By 1960, petroleum products, including natural gas, had toppled King Coal from its throne. Coal provided only 24.5 percent of energy used in the nation, with oil and natural gas providing 68.4 percent. Hydropower and fuel wood each supplied about 3.5 percent of U.S. energy consumed in 1960.

Most experts are in general agreement that these proportions are likely to hold in the immediate period ahead.

The change from wood to coal laid the basis for the growth of the iron and steel industry. Expanded steel production stimulated the construction of railroads throughout the country, metal machines of all kinds spurred the growth of mass production. New and cheaper sources of lubrication and illumination came from petroleum products.

During this century, liquid fuel and electricity have made possible even more changes. Lighting, communications and automatic controls and farm operations—all have been changed and reorganized. Liquid fuels have made possible the vast growth of automotive transportation and highway systems carrying motorized vehicles. Each innovation, each shift from older to newer energy forms—in combination with other changes—has transformed ways of living.

Next to water and air, upon which we depend for existence, energy is our most indispensable resource. Without it, an urbanized industrial society and today's manner of living would be impossible.

FUTURE ENERGY REQUIREMENTS

Since World War II, searching questions have been raised concerning future trends in the demand for energy. The aim is to ascertain the amounts necessary to maintain an adequate supply and establish the necessary policies and programs to secure it.

Since the landmark study of the energy and raw materials situation was presented to President Truman by his Materials Policy Commission (Paley Report) in 1952, a number of important analyses of the problem have been made. Studies have been conducted by the Senate Select Committee on Water Resources, the National Academy of Science, the Atomic Energy Commission, the National Fuels and Energy Study Group and others. The most ambitious attempt to update the far-reaching Paley Report was "Resources in America's Future," a 1963 study issued by Resources for the Future, a non-profit organization. The Federal Power Commission's National Power Survey was released in 1964.

Most previous forecasts of U.S. energy demands have been underestimates. Actual requirements, in particular that for electric energy and natural gas, have had a consistent habit of bursting the seams of nearly every forecast. Even now, many present estimates discount the possible future effect of nuclear energy as a competitive fuel on the demand for power.

In view of an increasing U.S. population which will reach about 300 million people by the year 2000, a doubling of per capita use of energy during the next 35 years, the total demand for coal, oil, natural gas and electric power will increase threefold by 2000. By that time, the demand for electric power may have quadrupled.

AVAILABLE ENERGY RESERVES

It is quite evident that it will be necessary to triple available energy supplies from coal, oil, natural gas, hydropower and nuclear fuels to carry out this nation's obligation to its domestic and foreign commitments and maintain an expanding economy for the rest of the 20th century.

Does America have enough energy fuels within its borders or available from other countries to go around?

One British Thermal Unit (BTU) is the amount of energy sufficient to heat one pound of water one degree fahrenheit. The 1962 Senate fuels and energy study indicated there are fossil fuel reserves (coal, oil and natural gas) of about 28-30 quintillion BTUs. One quintillion is expressed numerically as 1 followed by 18 zeros.

Using somewhat different definitions, the U.S. Department of Interior furnished the Atomic Energy Commission with energy reserve estimates used in the Commission's 1962 study on civilian nuclear power. Interior showed about 130 quintillion BTUs of fossil fuel energy reserves—6 quintillion were known and could be processed at about the same costs as those presently prevailing; 124 quintillion were in the form of marginal, more costly and inferred but not yet discovered resources. About 1.4 quintillion BTUs of energy resources had been consumed in America by 1962 and, by 2000, an estimated 5 quintillion BTUs will have been used up.

On this basis the U.S. will have depleted its presently known low-cost energy reserves within the next century or less and all foreseeable conventional energy resources within 150 to 200 years.

It should be kept in mind that all forecasts of energy consumption become less reliable the further into the future they attempt to penetrate.

Coal and petroleum resources are non-renewable; that is, they were formed by intense heat over millions of years. Each ton of coal mined, each barrel of oil or thousand cubic feet of natural gas extracted from wells reduces the national and world supply absolutely.

Yet estimates of available supplies of oil and natural gas are constantly being revised as new discoveries are made, both in the United States and abroad. The coal reserves of this country are still enormous and appear ample, for this century at least. The higher costs of the exploration and location of oil deposits and of mining lower grade coal at greater depths will tend to affect consumers in the years to come unless new techniques and devices offset this trend.

Competing new sources of energy inevitably will make it less desirable to expand exploration for new fossil fuels resources (coal and petroleum), even without taking into consideration the desirability of their wise conservation.

A tapering off of the heavy dependency on the use of these energy fuels long before the time of their exhaustion can be expected. During this period technological change within the fossil fuel industries will slow down the rate of their depletion and reduce the costs of their extraction, processing and transportation.

America, with only 6 percent of the world's population, contains about 30 percent of the world's supply of fossil fuels. While the world rate of energy use is about the same as that of the United States, it is depleting its less extensive reserves three times more rapidly.

For example, the United States has become a net importer of petroleum, obtaining about 20 percent of its requirements from abroad. This, however, reflects the lower world market cost of petroleum, not a present shortage of U.S. oil.

America's energy conservation position will not in the long run be aided by this growing dependence on foreign sources of oil. As industry and technology are accelerated in the developing nations, this will increase the world consumption of oil and other energy fuels, with foreign reserves becoming depleted before our own. This cannot but aggravate the strain on U.S. oil and coal deposits as they will be called upon for export. This situation requires swift steps to:

1. Supplement existing fossil fuels wherever economically-feasible new or supplementary energy fuels can be used on a meaningful scale;

2. Develop increasingly efficient methods of discovering, extracting, processing, transporting and using conventional, new and supplementary energy fuels;

3. Develop new and improve on present techniques of electric power generation and transmission.

Two new and enormous sources of energy are expected to play a significant part in achieving the goal of enlarging the resource base of America and the world within the next two or three decades or sooner.

The new energy sources are oil from shale rock and nuclear power derived from uranium and thorium.

THE NEW SHALE OIL RESOURCE

Beneath the plateau country of the Upper Colorado River Basin in portions of Colorado, Utah and Wyoming, lies the largest energy resource in the world—oil shale—containing a petroleum equivalent 40-fold larger than the nation's combined reserves of coal, liquid petroleum and natural gas. It is capable of meeting the future requirements of the United

States for the next two centuries and is conservatively worth between $2.5 and $5 trillion.

Eighty percent of the oil share potential is owned by the United States and administered by the Bureau of Land Management of the Department of Interior.

The emerging question is whether this enormous energy storehouse will be developed and controlled to benefit the nation or to enrich a handful of giant oil companies.

The efforts of labor, conservation, farm and consumer groups, have slowed down what appeared to be a fast takeover by the large oil companies, with the purpose of getting the oil shale lands and then developing them at their leisure and on their own terms. The Secretary of Interior, the Senate Interior Committee and the Senate Anti-Trust and Monopoly Subcommittee were warned by these groups that many basic questions need to be solved before development gets under way.

Oil shale rock has been used for heating and later for liquid petroleum for more than 125 years, particularly in high fuel cost areas in Europe, Asia, Australia and South Africa. Even now it is used for gas in heating in Estonia and Leningrad, USSR.

Although supplanted as an expanding energy source by the big oil discoveries in the U.S. and elsewhere, there was an intense and speculative boom shortly after World War I in Colorado, followed by enactment of the Minerals Leasing Act of 1920 which closed off filing of oil shale claims under the 1872 Mining Acts. In 1930, President Hoover withdrew all federal lands from oil shale development and, during the New Deal, President Roosevelt opened them up only for conventional oil, gas and sodium leasing.

The World War II petroleum shortages stimulated development by the Department of the Interior of a pilot oil shale program near Rifle, Colorado, to develop an economically competitive technology. This was abandoned under oil company pressures during the Eisenhower Administration and taken up again with the oil companies operating the facility under government contract during the Kennedy and Johnson administrations.

In 1963 and early 1964, the AFL-CIO informally urged the Secretary of the Interior to appoint a broad-based Oil Shale Advisory Committee, which released its report in 1965. The group agreed that the oil shale resource was immense and valuable, but split on policy and program of development, in particular the respective roles of the federal government and of industry.

In 1967, the Secretary announced a proposed 5-point development program, leading to fullscale commercial leasing. This program was opposed by labor, farm, consumer and conservation groups before hearings conducted in February and in May 1967, both by the Senate Interior Committee and the Anti-Trust and Monopoly Subcommittee of the Senate Judiciary Committee and under chairmanship of Senator Hart of Michigan.

In 1967, legislation was introduced in both the Senate and House to establish an orderly program of oil shale development in the public interest, a position supported by the AFL-CIO. Also that year, the Secretary announced that he would review his own proposals.

A modified set of program recommendations was issued by the Secretary on May 29, 1968. While modifying his 1967 program in some respects, these do not constitute an adequate program and continues its control squarely in the hands of the grandfather oil companies.

The problems facing oil shale development are complex and difficult, but not insuperable. First, the cloudy federal title to the old claims prior to 1966 and the thousands filed during 1966, allegedly for sodium minerals, must be resolved in the courts. Second, the oil shale resource and the intermixed sodium minerals must be explored and evaluated. Third, an effective technology or technologies must be established for mining, crushing and heating the rock to release the liquid kerogen, but at the same time observe conservation values. Fourth, major policies of leasing, or of federal yardstick demonstration plants, must be determined and with it an effort to benefit consumers by lower prices for petroleum products, and the establishment of a competitive oil shale industry, together with safeguards against its being taken over by the oil corporation giants.

The 1967 policy statement on oil shale adopted by the AFL-CIO called for an orderly federal multiple-use oil shale development program which would "develop economically competitive and feasible methods of processing oil shale, and other intermixed minerals, foster the development of a competitive oil shale industry, protect the environment affected by such programs, help provide abundant supplies of low-cost petroleum products to the American consumer, safeguard leasing arrangements against monopoly, and use revenues from any leasing program to assist in financing federal public sector programs."

The battle over control of one of the richest resources still belonging to the American people is only beginning. Its outcome will be of great importance to the future of every citizen and every worker.

THE NEW NUCLEAR RESOURCE

Nuclear energy in a power reactor provides heat which makes steam which in turn generates electric power, heats buildings and is useful in other industrial processes. Except for the kind of energy fuel used, there is no difference between nuclear heat and heat derived from burning coal, oil or natural gas.

Nuclear power has certain restrictions in the range of its applications. Unit costs are attractive only in large-scale power plants and ships. The reason for this is the indispensable need for massive and expensive shielding and elaborate safety devices and precautions to protect against the possibility of nuclear accidents. For reasons of safety, atomic power stations until recently have been placed at some distance from large concentrations of population.

The safety factor in plant location is becoming less and less a point of objection, with advancing knowledge and experience in operating reactors. Nevertheless, attempts by utilities to construct large nuclear power installations in such cities as New York and Los Angeles have met with strenuous opposition from local groups on safety grounds.

The means must be found to provide citizens with better information on nuclear power facilities and safety problems involved if public confidence is to be achieved and utilities enabled to add nuclear plants to their systems, observing all necessary safety criteria to protect the public.

There are areas such as New England, the Great Lakes region and California, where the costs of coal, natural gas and fuel oil are very high. It is in these areas that nuclear power is now competitive in the costs of generating electricity with conventional fossil fuels. In the future, nuclear power also should be able to compete with other energy sources in the heating of homes and office buildings.

ENVIRONMENTAL PROBLEMS

For many years, the Atomic Energy Commission has been developing experimental reactors of a design which will produce more nuclear fuel than is used in the generation of electricity. These are called breeder reactors.

The only breeder reactor now in commercial production is being operated on a test basis by a private power company near Detroit, Michigan.

It probably will be a matter of only a relatively few years before breeder reactors can be used by commercial electric utilities. They will make it possible to utilize the entire energy potential contained in uranium and thorium. This would mean the known nuclear resource would be increased by a factor of 100, making mining costs a negligible factor.

A breakthrough in breeder technology would open up for processing enormous quantities of low-grade uranium and thorium ore. Thorium is an element which yields a fissionable isotope of uranium (U-238). These elements are found in the granitic rocks of the Appalachian chain from New England to Tennessee, in the Rocky Mountains and the Great Lakes states and in phosphate and shale oil rock in the Rocky Mountains, in Tennessee and Florida.

In ultimate terms, uranium and thorium, if mined to fuel more and more breeder reactors of the future, would stupendously multiply the energy resources of America some 2,300 times. This would give substance to a prophecy made several years ago by Lewis Strauss, former AEC chairman, that one day nuclear power would be so cheap and abundant it would not even be metered.

In the last decade, the costs of generating a kilowatt-hour of electric power from a nuclear-fueled plant has dropped from more than 50 mills to between 8 to 14 mills. Plants now under construction or planned will hopefully bring costs down to somewhere between 4 to 7 mills, fully competitive in many areas with large unit coal-fired power stations.

It must be remembered, however, that the long-range future of nuclear power does not lie with burner reactors now in use but with the breeders, simply on the basis of fully utilizing the resource. The value of the present generation of atomic power plants is mainly in high fuel cost areas, with great promise if employed in huge units of a million kilowatts or more to generate both for power and large-scale desalinization of water in the southwestern and Gulf states and water-short regions elsewhere in the world. Work on this most important aspect of peaceful nuclear development is already proceeding with joint cooperation between the AEC and the Interior Department, with international scientific collaboration between the U.S. and Israel and the United States and the Soviet Union.

If shale oil and nuclear resources are brought into full play in serving the expanding energy requirements of a still increasing population in a full employment economy, they will provide an immense base from which the United States economy can rise to new heights.

The expansion of the utility industry even now accounts for about 10 percent of total national industrial construction. By 1980, its annual capital investment is expected to reach some $6.5 billion and, by the end of the century, $20 billion. Annual costs of generating and transmitting electric power may exceed $15 billion by 1980 and approach $50 billion by 2000.

Reductions in nuclear power costs would not only serve as healthy competition to coal and natural gas, but could largely eliminate the now significant differences in fuel costs between regions because of transportation costs and thus save consumers billions of dollars in power bills each year.

Moreover, expansion of shale oil uses will enable more effective conservation of conventional petroleum resources. In the same manner, the use of nuclear power to produce electricity will aid in conservation of coal reserves and stimulate research and development into other potential uses of coal—as a liquid fuel and in industrial processes—which would be non-competitive with nuclear energy.

With strong regulation through the federal power yardstick, there could be a lower rate base and lower bills for the nation's electricity users. It would be possible to sell power at prices not much higher than the costs of transmission, operation, maintenance and replacement.

Such low costs could be expected to produce a soaring per capita use of electricity. Over the nation generally, but in particular in regions now penalized by higher energy fuel costs, industrial development would gain momentum.

Overcrowded and decaying urban centers could be decentralized, with populations gathered around nuclear energy complexes which would create power and expand other uses of nuclear energy. This would help create better towns and cities, better use of land and reduce the strain on transportation facilities.

NEW GENERATION AND TRANSMISSION TECHNIQUES

In recent years, space and military research programs have developed a new concept of power generation—the direct conversion of the chemical energy of heat releases to electric energy. The aim of this research is to eliminate steam boilers, turbines and generators in the production of electric power.

Among the methods of direct generation being pursued is the thermo-electric generator, which enables electricity to be passed off into a wire from application of heat to electric conductors.

In the field of transportation, fuel cells bear great promise. They differ from the ordinary storage battery principle in that the energy is provided by chemical reaction and is not stored. The Tennessee Valley Authority has been experimenting with an auto powered by a fuel cell, with only 30-odd moving parts. Longer lasting fuel cells could provide a basis for a profound revolution in the petroleum and automobile industries.

Thermonuclear fusion power is based on the principle of releasing tremendous quantities of energy by combining lighter elements at high velocity to form new and heavier elements.

The world's nuclear scientists have been at work on the problem of containment of plasma in a magnetic field at temperatures between 40 to 100 million degrees centigrade in order to provide a sustained reaction emitting energy.

The heavy hydrogen atoms (deuterium and tritium) used in this technique are found throughout the world's oceans and seas. Success in achieving fusion power would place still another energy resource of almost inconceivable vastness at the disposal of the people of the world in the more distant future.

The technology of efficiently transmitting huge amounts of power over distances up to 1,000 miles or more has been designated as ehv (extra heavy voltage). More familiarly, when combined with huge coal or atomic-fueled generating plants, it is known as "giant power."

The giant power concept was pioneered by the late Gifford Pinchot in the 1920s. It was utilized in the early English power grid and by TVA and the Bonneville Power Administration during the 1930s and 1940s.

But since that time various European countries, including the USSR, have expanded ehv to carry 500,000 volts or more of electric energy, as compared to the 345,000 volt lines of TVA and Bonneville.

The federal power agencies and private utilities of this country, however, are now expanding ehv in earnest. A vast system of ehv lines to exchange power between the Pacific Northwest and the Pacific Southwest to the Mexican border is well toward completion. Utilities, singly or in loosely-associated groups, are now exploring ehv.

The result most certainly will be regional, interregional power exchanges and finally a national power supply system. The thermal plants would supply the steady power demand, while hydro plants would be operated to meet sudden load demands of users.

The 1964 National Power Survey of the Federal Power Commission set forth the needs and advantages of such mixed ownership networks and suggested that it could result by 1980 in savings of fixed charges amounting to some $11.7 billion a year for the nation—much of which could be passed on to the consumer in the form of lower electricity bills.

The national concern over the two major power failures of 1965 and 1967 which affected millions of citizens, resulted in FPC and administration proposed legislation to ensure reliability of electrical service and avoid major blackouts (the Electric Power Reliability Act of 1967). Legislation has also been introduced to require private utilities building nuclear plants to allow smaller consumer owned utilities to buy into them and thus obtain an adequate future power supply. Increasing attention is now being given by the Federal Power Commission as to the effects of transmission lines on the environment and of nuclear plants on thermal pollution.

As the nation's largest consumers' organization, the AFL-CIO is vitally interested that the fruits of such a new advance will be reflected both in abundant supplies of power and lower power bills. It is equally interested to assist in developing national policies designed to prevent monopoly control.

Today's need is for broad energy planning and policy decisions made at the national level and geared both to immediate and longer range national objectives of strengthening economic growth and stability. All such policies should embody widespread benefits to consumers, safeguards against growth of monopoly and employment of wise conservation, management and use, including the control of adverse environmental effects.

Not only must man use these forces for his release from the fetters of his natural environment, but he must come to understand that the forces he now controls have become so enormous and so impersonal that they are impacting his physical habitat and his social organization as well. The crucial task ahead is to find ways to harmonize the polarized extremes of the natural system of evolution and the deliberate manipulation of natural evolutionary processes by man. Human freedom and human wellbeing depend on how well this challenge is met.

Basic Approaches to the Solution

WHAT ARE THE PRACTICAL ASPECTS OF SOLVING
THE ENVIRONMENTAL CRISIS? WHY ARE THERE NO
SIMPLISTIC SOLUTIONS?

How should we approach the problem of understanding
man and his environment as integral parts of an ecosystem?

What should be the role of the universities in environmental
study and action?

What fundamental legal concepts need to be revised in the
light of environmental issues?

What lessons can citizens and government learn from the
case history of Cayuga Lake?

What new kind of industrial revolution is now needed?

How could a city be designed to preserve and enhance the
quality of the human environment?

A phenomenon of our time is the worldwide realization that man is inexorably restricted by ecological laws. He has suddently realized on a worldwide scale that his lack of concern for these laws can terminate his species, just as the great reptiles disappeared as their position deteriorated millions of years ago. Although civilizations in the past have succumbed to, or collapsed from, violations of their ecological situation, it has been the great increases in our numbers and the explosive rise in the effectiveness of our technology that have brought the full import of those principles on human survival and the resulting dilemma of survival to practically universal attention.

Orme Lewis, Jr.

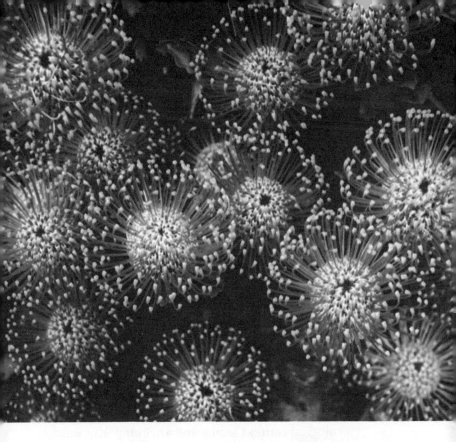

Ecosystem Science as a Point of Synthesis

S. Dillon Ripley
Helmut K. Buechner

The most critical problem facing humanity today is an ecological one of relating human societies harmoniously to their environments. Before conditions caused by radioactive fallout, pollution, exploding populations, the greenhouse effect of increased atmospheric carbon dioxide, and inter-societal aggression can be treated, the knowledge of the humanities and the behavioral sciences, as well as the natural sciences, must be integrated. Our recent awareness of critical environmental problems has created a favorable climate of thought for an intellectual orientation of knowledge relevant to contemporary world problems. But the task of orienting knowledge in a contemporary ecological context seems overwhelming. Knowledge has become so complex that depth of understanding requires specialization. Appreciable understanding of other disciplines is often necessary to a satisfying performance in a given specialty, but comprehension of the unity of knowledge appears difficult to achieve.

An idea for orienting knowledge on an ecological theme in a context of today's world problems is suggested by the concepts of "levels of biological integration" and "points of view," and their philosophic basis, formulated by Frank E. Egler twenty-five years ago.[1] The levels of integration are now so widely accepted that this approach has been incorporated into the BSCS series of high-school textbooks. The points of view, however, have not had a comparable impact.

134

Although this system for organizing knowledge was already established in Europe during the nineteenth century, its use in American research and education has been casual and seemingly without full awareness of its value. Our purpose in the present paper is to present a two-dimensional conceptual model, based on levels of integration and points of view, as an aid in orienting knowledge with relevance to the ecological crisis.

The first dimension of the model considers levels of biological integration in terms of ecosystems. Biological entities, such as cells, organisms, populations, and communities, represent levels of integration in which the whole is more than a mere sum of the parts. A population of an African antelope, for example, has a birth rate, a death rate, a social behavior, an intrinsic rate of population increase, and a pool of genetic variation—all attributes that emerge at the population level of integration through the interactions of the individual members. By integrating the population of antelopes with all other kinds of living organisms and the nonliving, or physical, components (such as earth, water, and air), a more complex level of organization emerges, to which the term *ecosystem* has been applied. An ecosystem, or ecological system, functions as an interacting whole in nature. It is an open-energy system in which solar energy is incorporated into organic compounds through the photosynthetic process in green plants. Energy circulates within the plant, from plant to animal, from animal to animal, and finally through decomposing organisms, such as fungi and bacteria. In this process, the original potential energy in plants is degraded from concentrated form to greater and greater dispersion as unavailable heat energy, until all of it is lost to the living systems. An ecosystem is somewhat analogous to an open reservoir, with energy in place of water flowing through the system. Maintaining the ecosystem requires a constant input of energy, which moves through the system and is eventually lost to the system. Through feedback mechanisms, the system maintains a certain degree of stability in what is known as a steady state, or homeostasis. A single cell and its microenvironment, whether free-living or part of a tissue system, may be conceptualized as an ecosystem. If viruses and rickettsiae are accepted as living systems, one can go to biological levels below that of the cell. Tissues, organs, organisms, populations of organisms of a single kind, interspecific populations of plants or animals, and biocommunities constitute biological entities at levels of increasing complexity; each can be considered an ecosystem if the total environment is added as an integral part of the system.

Populations of human beings are uniquely characterized by their highly complex social behavior, which emerges as human society. The societies of man, together with their total environments, form the highest level of biological integration, the emergent attributes of which are incomparably more complex than those of a population of an African antelope. Man's societies dominate all ecosystems on earth. The current ecological crisis arises out of this dominance, since man has allowed his populations to increase excessively and to degrade his environmental systems.

We need to concentrate our orientation of knowledge on the human-society-plus-environment level of integration because of its relevance to the central world problem of achieving a reasonably steady state between human societies and the finite resources of our planet. We are as much concerned with human society itself as with the environments in which men live; both are parts of an interacting whole that evolves as a unit through time.

The second dimension in our conceptual model concerns the points of view suggested in 1910 by S. Tschulok, and slightly modified by Egler, for studying any subject matter. Although the interfaces between points of view are increasingly recognized as significant areas of study, the separate points of view provide the basic framework for organizing knowledge. Any entity—be it a purely physical system, a biological organism, or a complex of any kind—may be studied from the following points of view:

1. The components of the system—sub-atomic particles, cells, living organisms, physical components (such as air and water) or planets of a solar system

2. Structure or morphology—the organization of the parts, including the social organization within and between species of animals, the structural relationships of plants in the physiognomy of vegetation, or the cells and organs of higher plants and animals

3. Functions and processes—the physiology of the system, including regulatory mechanisms that control homeostasis in living systems at any level of organization

4. Distribution in time—changes in the system through time, whether ontogenetic or phylogenetic

5. Distribution in space—zoogeography, phytogeography, or human geography, for example

6. Relationships to environment—the influence of the entity on the environment as well as the environmental effects on the entity

7. Classification—for example, the taxonomy of plants or animals, the classification of vegetation, or the classification of whole ecosystems

These points of view can be applied to the human-society-plus-environment level of integration. At this level, as at any other, there are unique attributes for the system as a whole. The movement of radioactive particles or DDT through plants and nonhuman animals into man—who released these contaminants in the first place—is an ecosystem phenomenon.

It involves decisions in the minds of men as well as the physical movement of the particles through the air, water, and soil. Through the past five thousand years, man has been altering his environments to his own disadvantage—as in the salinization of the soils of Mesopotamia, the deforestation of Iran and Greece, the overgrazing by sheep in Spain, the destruction of the Great Lakes fisheries by the sea lamprey, the drying-up of the Everglades National Park, the expansion of the arid lands of the world, pollution of rivers, the eutrophication of lakes and estuaries, the excessive erosion of topsoil from our most valuable arable lands, and the atmospheric pollution in Los Angeles. Modern technology provides the capacity for macroenvironmental manipulations unimagined a few years ago. Man's alterations of planet earth are phenomena of ecosystems at the level of human-society-plus-environment. They involve new processes, resulting from the behavior of man, that were not part of the physiology of the earth's ecosystems five thousand years ago.

It is important to recognize that human societies are an integral component of the highest level of biological integration. Man is in nature; he is a part of nature, not a separate and divine creation acting as an outside influence on the earth's ecosystems. The impact of man on natural systems is mediated through human societies. Societies themselves are complex, integrated wholes with unique characteristics that emerge from the interactions of individual human beings. Mob violence or peaceful civil rights demonstrations exhibit characteristics not expressed by man as an individual. Similarly, the making of decisions that affect society is normally a phenomenon of group action. The U.S. Congress represents something more than a mere summation of the individual thoughts of congressmen. The quality of the individuals that constitute society and the groups within societies naturally determines the behavior of society as a whole. One person can have a significant influence on society, as in the case of Rachel Carson through her book *The Silent Spring.*

Society can be conceptually segregated from the natural ecosystem for the purpose of studying its unique attributes, although society is, in fact, a component of a larger whole and the segregation is an artificial one. The study of society from the seven points of view mentioned earlier provides a perspective on the role of the social scientist and humanist in reaching an understanding of the total system of human-society-plus-environment.

Man's image of the world in which he lives and his understanding of man's place in the universe are critical in achieving ecological homeostasis. Science can contribute basic facts and ideas about ecosystems. But man's concerns and values also determine the behavior of societies. His conceptual environment has changed through time, a transformation expressed in literature, poetry, music, architecture, and modifications of the landscape. The natural scientist will most probably have less influence in the evolution of a conceptual environment relevant to today's ecological crisis than the humanist. Man's conceptual environment, not science, will determine the future of humanity.

The humanist now has the responsibility of developing our understanding of values with relevance to the central ecological problems of our times. Seemingly, an ecological theme in which one studies the history of man in the context of his environmental relationships can be as fundamental and intellectually rewarding as a traditional approach through the cultural evolution of man with emphasis on political systems. Instead of studying society isolated in a historical context, one should study the whole ecosystem of human-society-plus-environment and the interrelationships between these systems on a global basis. By segregating society from the rest of the natural system, the behavioral scientist and humanist can perhaps more readily identify his role in helping to achieve a steady state, but ultimately they must integrate society and man's total environment into an ecosystem concept.

Ecosystems at the highest level of biological integration are not only more complex than we think they are, but more complex than we *can* think. Thus, we can never achieve a total understanding of the human-society-plus-environment system. Nevertheless, the two-dimensional conceptual model suggested here does provide an approach through which interdisciplinary efforts can be organized to evolve unifying principles and concepts leading to a better understanding of man's place in the universe. In this model, the human-society-plus-environment ecosystem represents a point of synthesis for the focus of research and education on the contemporary problems of adapting human societies harmoniously to their environments. The orientation of knowledge necessary to achieve a self-sustaining homeostasis of human societies within the ecosystems of the world is the responsibility not only of university scientists and educators, but also of scientists in private corporations and government agencies, congressmen, city planners, musicians, landscape architects—indeed, all individuals and groups that can contribute effectively in a common effort ranging from the pure theory of ecosystem-oriented science to its application.

How can we come to grips with the formidable task of achieving an ecological orientation before irreversible alterations in our ecosystems preclude the evolution of higher levels of human life? Our universities are at the heart of the advancement of knowledge in the separate disciplines, but their administrative structure tends to militate against the interdisciplinary programs. Students and higher administrators may be ready for a contemporary ecological orientation for education and research, but many university scholars were programmed before the space age, and for some, reprogramming is impossible. Many government agencies are filled with mission-oriented bureaucrats and scientists who fight for their projects like department heads at universities. Fortunately, the educated public is becoming more and more concerned with the problems of the atomic bomb and pollutants. There is a gnawing feeling that we cannot know the safe levels of DDT and strontium 90 without more basic research over a significant period of time. Many congressmen, expressing concern over the quality of our environment, are ready to tackle such fundamental problems—problems left untouched in the past.

The task involves research, education, and communication of information to society. The solution of our problems in agriculture resulted in large part from the remarkable feedback system at our land-grant colleges, in which all three of these components were present. Compared with agriculture, the problem of bringing the world's exploding populations into homeostasis within the limited natural resources is infinitely more challenging. Perhaps we can develop the organizational structure we need at regional centers for ecosystem science, which would emphasize interdisciplinary approaches and use the human-society-plus-environment ecosystem as a point of synthesis. Such centers for ecosystem science are needed not only in the United States, but in other strategic regions of the world. Initially, the body of basic knowledge required for ecological homeostasis must be accumulated. But subsequently, education and the flow of sound information to the general public will be vital to rapid progress and ultimate success. In research, the guidance of our best scholars in science, technology, social science, and the humanities is needed so that knowledge meaningful in the context of time and relevant to our ecological crisis will evolve. Our critical shortage of professional ecologists and the urgency of orienting general education to an ecological theme define the problem in education. Since society will ultimately determine the future of our ecosystems, the decisions of society require an ecological basis that can be developed only through communication of sound knowledge to the general public. Special centers for advanced studies focusing attention on the critical problems of man's ecological behavior can enhance the programs at regional centers in the major ecosystems of the world.

Regional centers must involve universities, but because the centers are new and organized on an integrative theme, they will provide opportunities for developing interdisciplinary programs without being hampered by the conventional departmental structure of universities. Strong financial support from Congress would preclude the struggle for survival among departments or disciplines. The co-operation of universities, governmental laboratories, federal agencies, industry, and private foundations is essential to such regional centers. Each organization will have clearly identified roles and indispensable functions. The value of the Smithsonian Institution as a basically private organization with strong governmental relationships should not be overlooked by society.

By recognizing that human societies and their total environments form the highest level of biological integration, one can direct thought and research to the unique phenomena that emerge at this level in nature. By approaching the human-society-plus-environment ecosystem as a whole, the special disciplines of knowledge are more precisely revealed in their relationship to one another and to the entire scope of man's knowledge. A more profound ecological knowledge of man-in-nature, developed through the two-dimensional model suggested here and others, is fundamental to higher levels of human life and meaning—both in respect to the quality of human individuals and human societies and to the symbolic expression of these values in the external landscape.

REFERENCES

1. Frank E. Egler, "Vegetation as an Object of Study," *Philosophy of Science*, Vol. 9, No. 3 (1942), pp. 245-60.
2. S. Tschulok, "Das System der Biologie," ed., Forschung and Lehr, *Eine historisch kritische Studie* (Jena, 1910).

There must be interdisciplinary inquiry into the relations of knowledge to wise ethical and technical choices, and into the possibilities of a world aesthetically, socially, and ecologically more satisfactory than the present one. An exploration of the significance of the work in the disciplines for the actions of various leaders in society must be part of the legitimate long-run research and scholarship of the faculty. Ways must be found, on an interdisciplinary basis, for comparing quantifiable variables of economic cost with the less quantifiable variables of beauty and well-being, as for example the comparison of the economic costs of clear skies, clean water, pleasing architecture, and accessible wilderness with the human satisfactions of living in such an environment.

New Wine

How Should
the University
Treat Environment?

F. Kenneth Hare

I was asked this question recently by a group at a major American university, and I have spent a long time pondering it. What should be the scope of environmental studies? How should they be organized? What is the relation between the political interest in environment and the things that make sense on the campus? I believe that we can answer these questions only if we are willing to poke hard at the university's cherished myths, and that we shall not make any sense politically until we have sorted ourselves out. The climate of the times demands that we do make political sense.

I had read an illuminating study of the political implications of concern for the environment (1), and in August I had the chance of listening to a discourse Caldwell gave privately (2). Although silent during the discussion that followed, I responded next day with an open letter to Caldwell's host, C. P. Runge, who has allowed me to amplify this letter into an article for wider circulation. I am not the first person to be set in motion by Caldwell's clarity and realism. In spite of his involvement in congressional affairs he looks at the question as I think all academics must—as one that we cannot ignore.

I will look mainly at the question of environmental studies in large, structurally complex universities like those spread widely over the Middle West. We all know the conservative quality of such places, where nothing can easily be done for either the first or the last time. The status quo is defended in depth by the vested interests of a large number of able people. Among these interests are those of the traditional departments and the largely analytical disciplines they profess. Also strong are the numerous special institutes and centers that have gotten started in spite of the resistance of the departments. When we propose to start up a broad-spectrum, synthesizing effort like environmental studies we run full tilt into all these vested interests.

We also bang ourselves against the clan spirit of the traditional faculty groupings. Humanists, social scientists, natural scientists, and professionals like lawyers and engineers may fight like cats within the clan, but they close ranks and hitch up their kilts when someone questions their loyalties. Environmental studies have to involve many of these clans, which are not used to combining in the way required. If we suggest, as I do, that some of them—notably the humanists—may be utterly transformed by such combinations, we alarm the timid and anger the Tories among them.

But the greatest hazard in our path is inherent in Lyndon Johnson's acid query "Therefore, what?," which he is said to have thrown at a group of professors who had just briefed him on the Middle Eastern situation. The political interest in the environment demands proposals for *action*—on all time scales, from the immediate assault on pollution problems and other festering sores of today, to the long-term reconstruction of society in a better relation with environment. At present we are not equipped to make such proposals. We are not action-oriented, and on every campus there is a deadweight of opinion that regards action-oriented programs as hostile to the academic life.

In many ways this fear is justified. Being action-oriented, getting ourselves involved in planning society's future, and mending its present broken bones, does indeed threaten the selfish individualism and pursuit of our own private thing that we call academic freedom. If we take on the job outlined by Caldwell, we must have a lot more institutional discipline. If the university as a whole adopts social goals of this kind, we must accept a greater degree of common directed action—of teamwork—than we are used to in most faculties. Doctors and engineers do this all the time. It will be in the humanities and social science areas where the shock will be most felt, because these are the chief homes of the lone wolf *(3)*.

I must also stress the incompetence of the established disciplines to tackle many of society's real problems. What we mean by a discipline is an agreed, tested body of method—usually analytical—that we bring to bear on problems of our own choosing. The essence of our thinking is that we cannot tackle problems that do not fit the competence of our own discipline. It is true that we constantly try to enlarge that competence. Confronted with a new problem, we spare no effort to improve our methods. But if we do not succeed, we do not tackle the problem, and we tend to condemn colleagues who try.

Public policy—such as environmental control and design policies—can never insulate itself in this way. It has to face the real problems as they present themselves in all their complexity, and policy makers have to act on highly inadequate preparation and incomplete evidence. Policy-making is a crude process in which synthesis or just guesswork precedes accurate analysis. Moreover, it is nearly always broad spectrum in character, because no important social problem is ever simple and none ever lies fully within the competence of a single academic discipline. Even such questions as monetary and fiscal policy contain large components outside economics. We therefore arrive at the pessimistic conclusions that (i) the existing departmental and disciplinary structure of the university is out of kilter with the needs of action-oriented, policy-directed programs, and that (ii) we do not yet know how to adapt ourselves to this sort of challenge. We shall have to change, in fact, without knowing how to start.

What change, and how do we bring it off?

Our usual response is to say, "We are dealing with an interdisciplinary problem"; or, like the American Water Resources Association, "a multidisciplinary problem." In the past 20 years North American universities have said this many thousands of times. The result has been the proliferation of institutes, centers, programs, and so forth, dedicated to some problem, usually dominated by an individual with an idea, and legitimized by a committee. Most of these ventures have a short life, and most fail to survive the departure of the dominant individual. We can easily see that the step toward environmental studies is another and very ambitious move of this kind, and we must stop to ask ourselves the larger question—how do we create a more stable kind of interdisciplinary organism? *(4)*.

The answer, I suggest, is that the study of problems such as we have been discussing is not simply interdisciplinary in the sense that it involves several of the old disciplines. Instead it demands a new kind of discipline, basically synthesizing in method. I am sure that the university will have to answer more and more calls to solve social problems, and that, if we do not answer these calls, we shall be bypassed by the creation of new kinds of institutions more flexible and realistic in outlook. I conclude that we must learn to develop these new disciplines of synthesis, and make them as rigorous as the older analytical disciplines. I can hear the scoffers scoffing—but, if we do not tackle this, we shall deserve to be counted out. By all means let us encourage interdisciplinary ventures—but in the hope that they will indeed become disciplines of the new kind.

I am aware that this is a gross oversimplification. No discipline is ever wholly analytic or wholly synthetic. None is completely logical and consistent in its methods. It is clear nonetheless that chemistry and physics are quite different from geography and history. The first two characteristically isolate phenomena and study them as exactly as they can under close experimental control; the second two take the world as it comes—or as it came—and necessarily deal with a complex of things and events. As a geographer I have recently been feeling, ironically, that the tide of events is turning my way. My colleagues and I have been trying for a century to deal with a problem that is now announced as new—the study of man in his environmental setting.

There are, that is to say, a few of the broad disciplines already, and there are moves toward more. Systems thinking is popular, and the jargon of systems analysis even more so. Among many of the new social quantifiers the word "synthesis" is regarded with contempt; "multivariate analysis" sounds better. I suggest that the past century was the era in which we achieved great things by dissecting reality so that we could look at its fine texture; and that is how most of our existing disciplines got going. The next century will be that in which we learn to cope intellectually with complexes of things, and especially with those that make up the environment of man.

ORGANIZATION

Turning now to organization, I agree with Caldwell and others who say that success in environmental studies depends on the will to do it rather than on specific structural changes. What such ventures need are dedicated charismatic leaders, well known and respected on the campus, who will set out to create this will. I do not think that a massive before-the-fact recasting of the academic façade will achieve anything, and, unless you are in a very untypical university, it will engender factional opposition. So why not proceed informally?

If you decide to take the plunge, I suggest you gather round you all the like-minded members of the university you can find. Do not call yourselves a committee—be like the most successful scientific society I know, the Friends of the Pleistocene, which I believe has no officers, no journal, no headquarters, no subscription—but lots of members and solid achievement. The group or cabal (a term I favor) ought to point to its own most galvanic member and say, "You are it!" And he in turn ought to be trusted to go to Washington to fight for funds, having first got the pledges he needs from those willing to help. If you succeed and in 2 or 3 years have begun to get solid results, it ought to be easier to persuade other groups on the campus to join in.

SCOPE

And finally, the question of scope. This is difficult, because without even trying you can relate nearly everything to the theme "man and environment." The scope of an academic program in environmental studies has to be broad enough to catch the imagination of faculty and students, but narrow enough to avoid differences. It also has to be clearly related to social goals, for reasons of conscience as well as fund-raising.

At the outset I make the distinction between (i) short-term correction of technological errors, broadly "pollution control," and (ii) long-term design and control of the environment. The first is often summarized as "environmental quality," though this is a misnomer. I object also to the notion of "restoring the quality," because we should have to go too far back in time to do it—at least to the Neolithic.

The short-term problem of pollution control is as far as present-day public concern goes, except for certain farsighted men in and out—mostly out—of the universities. The Tukey Report of 1965 (5) defines this problem concisely; the report admits that Western industrial societies have made a mess of their own home, partly because human beings are just messy, but also because of the overconfident use of technological aids such as pesticides, the profligate overuse of resources like water, and the burning of fossil fuels. This has messed up America, and threatens to mess up the world. The report makes 104 sweeping recommendations for action, adding that this is an incomplete list, and publishes valuable appendices that offer the most authoritative review of the pollution problem. Hardly any of the recommendations have been acted upon, though they have had some effect on government practices.

It is quite clear that many of the problems defined by the authors of the Tukey report can be tackled by the universities. They stress the need for graduates trained in the necessary skills and fired with a concern for environmental restoration. Many of the specific recommendations touch on the need for the universities to undertake research and research-training in the field. It is also clear that the large modern university can be and already is involved in tackling the ad hoc problems enumerated in the report.

I do not, however, believe that a major university can sweepingly alter its work and outlook by adopting such a negative theme as the correction of past error. Something altogether more exciting and far reaching is needed. I look for this in the idea that in future we shall increasingly control and design our environment. We live in an era when we can extend our horizons for such control from the walls of our house to the ends of the earth. It will take time, but I have no doubt that we can and must convert this planet, not into a spaceship, which it already is, but into a safer and more comfortable home for our whole species and for the other living things with whom we coexist—and without whom, of course, we could neither eat nor breathe.

Boulding has argued that economics and ecology must come together; otherwise ecology is only bird-watching and egg-snatching, and economics continues to be dismal *(6)*. We have to earn our living by seeing to it that the rest of the living world can survive, too.

If we take this long-term, exalted view, how do we define environment? From a man's-eye view we can perceive these possibilities: (i) The natural environment, which means the physical-biotic world outside society, and our interactions with it. This view supposes that it is feasible to separate our handiwork from that of nature. It is the view that President Johnson took when he established the Environmental Science Services Administration. In his message he spoke of a unified treatment of the natural environment *(7)*. It is also the logic behind the creation in 1965 of Britain's Natural Environment Research Council, though I can testify as a founding member of that body that it took my colleagues a good while before they would have admitted, by majority vote, that a unified treatment of the environment was a useful exercise *(8)*. (ii) The social environment, which arises from the obvious fact that each of us has to survive in a matrix of our fellow men, and that each society must coexist with surrounding societies. In practice for most of us this means the problems of the Western city, with its nightmare inadequacies. On a world scale it must also mean the tensions of rural India and Pakistan, the Red Guards of Maoist China, and the tribal strife of some African countries. Nearly all the deepseated political problems of the world reside here. It is often argued that a major function of environmental design must be to reduce these tensions—as, for example, in the rebuilding of city centers. (iii) The built environment, which recognizes that man-made structures provide the actual home of both working and sleeping mankind, and in the richer societies that it also accommodates his play, his higher culture (whatever that may mean), and his vulgarities. Geographers have long talked about the cultural landscape, meaning that the built element in environment extends to the countryside. Landscape architects have a similar concern. (iv) Finally, there is the total environment, which pops up in the more exalted literature, and which seems to mean (i) + (ii) + (iii).

The trouble with such concepts is that the thing environed gets so mixed up with the environment that they become rather fuzzy.

I am not sure that we ought not to add to this list the spatial or geographic environment, in which (i), (ii), and (iii) occur intermixed, but are sufficiently spread out to be manageable. Certainly the environment of the ecologically minded geographer is a rather different thing from the sum of the components of the natural environment.

In many universities that have launched environmental studies, there is only provision to look after the natural environment, and the grouping consists of various interested parties in the physical and biological sciences, sometimes with the geographers thrown in. In others, the entire enterprise is given a strongly ecological twist. In still others the emphasis is upon planning, and the prime movers are architects. The number of open options is large, but one rarely finds a case where a university has committed itself deeply to a broadly based curriculum. In all cases known to me these are new universities—Wisconsin at Green Bay, East Anglia (U.K.), and Waterloo (Ontario), for example. In these places, environmental studies have been elevated to a par with arts, science, and the other traditional faculties. This is easy when the world seems young.

I assume that in major, highly evolved centers, where the great strength lies in the diversity of research skills and in the numbers of first-rate thinkers in the relevant disciplines, the starting point should be in research and graduate training. The enterprise's sponsors ought to start out by saying something like the following:

> 1. The university considers that the study of man's environment, natural, social, built, and complex, presents a splendid focus for future academic development. It not only touches on a life-and-death problem for the supporting society, but

opens up new lines of intellectual experiment that ought to keep us busy for a generation or more.

2. The framework of a unified program of environmental studies is ecological in the largest sense. It is made up of the links that in the real world connect a man's work and play with the people that surround him, his society with neighboring societies, and human society at large with the rest of the natural world. These links allow flows of energy and mass between domains, the kind of thing that some ecologists deal with in the ecology of biota. They also represent, for those connecting man with man directly, links in some kind of intellectual domain; if I were as obscure as Teilhard, I would call these the strands of the noosphere. And finally, and in concrete terms, the links represent, for civilized as well as barbarous societies, lines along which some of man's most important institutions must operate. We have achieved the proper outlook for environmental studies when and if we can see, or to want to see, these links in a unified ecological framework.

3. We have to admit that our viewpoint is that of Western industrialized society, and that we shall be working out our program in the light of that society's past mistakes and assumptions for its own future. This implies (i) that the Western value system is of direct concern to us, and that humanists ought to be deeply involved in environmental studies; and (ii) that we must not make the mistake of assuming that other societies have similar relations with environment, nor should they be expected to have Westernized ambitions

for the future. Rather, in fact, the reverse. It should be a major objective of those involved in environmental studies to alter the Western outlook on such questions. We shall solve our environmental problems only by deepseated changes in society itself.

4. Given that we achieve this altered outlook, it still seems likely that Western society will become even more completely urbanized in the future. It is hence necessary that the social sciences and psychology play a major role in environmental studies. The field of urban and regional planning is equally central, though I share Boulding's feeling that much of what we have done in these areas is well-meant error *(9)*. I think it is clear, nevertheless, that we shall increasingly try to deliberately design and build our future environment: and the core of our program should be a painstaking attempt to create a better atmosphere for such conscious creation.

5. Putting environmental theory into practice means political action, and the evolution of institutions to cope with the new ideas and requirements. Hence we can not hope to succeed without political scientists like Caldwell, institutions like Resources for the Future and the Conservation Foundation, and concerned public figures.

All this adds up to the fact that a really positive and successful program of environmental studies ought to involve a large part of the university, and it ought to spread downward until it contributes heavily to the undergraduate curriculum and influences what is done in the schools.

REFERENCES AND NOTES

1. L. K. Caldwell, in *Future Environments of North America*, F. F. Darling and J. P. Milton, Eds. (Natural History Press, New York, 1969), pp. 648-671.
2. I owe a debt to C. P. Runge, and to C. A. Engman, R. Bryson, and V. R. Potter (Univ. of Wisconsin) for many discussions of this subject, and for permission to publish this article.
3. At least one graduate dean, on hearing me express this view, says that engineers are as troublesome as the rest of us!
4. I realized this point only after discussion with Bryson and Potter. See also V. R. Potter, *Land Econ.* 38(1), 1 (1962).
5. J. W. Tukey, chairman, and Environmental Panel, President's Science Advisory Committee, report, *Restoring the Quality of Our Environment* (White House, Washington, D.C., 1965).
6. K. E. Boulding, in *Future Environments of North America*, F. F. Darling and J. P. Milton, Eds. (Natural History Press, New York, 1966), pp. 225-234.
7. L. B. Johnson, letter of transmittal to the Congress, on Reorganization Plan No. 2, 1965, the United States Weather Bureau. See *Bull. Amer. Meteorol. Soc.* 46, 457 (1965).
8. I compared the two bodies in F. K. Hare, *Geography* 51(2), 99 (1966).
9. K. E. Boulding, in *Future Environments of North America*, F. F. Darling and J. P. Milton, Eds. (Natural History Press, New York, 1966), pp. 291-292.

This world of ours is a new world, in which the unity of knowledge, the nature of human communities, the order of society, the order of ideas, the very notions of society and culture have changed, and will not return to what they have been in the past.

J. Robert Oppenheimer

From Conservation to
Environmental Law
David Sive

If environmental issues are to dominate the seventies as civil rights and racial equality dominated the sixties, one of the critical questions is whether the courts will play an equally important role. If they do, fundamental concepts of private property rights will have to be reexamined in the light of the basic ecological teaching that one man's toilet is another man's faucet. The philosophy of the frontier still underlies most doctrines of land and water rights and duties.

Despite the absence of clearly applicable constitutional phrases or clauses—such as "due process," "equal protection" and "privileges and immunities" in civil rights causes—the coming and imminent explosion in the courts is clearly in the field of environmental law.

The certainty is based on two separate trails of history, one political and one judicial. The political side is documented daily in every newspaper and news magazine. To young and old, left and right, wilderness hiker and urbanite, the environment is the "in" subject. Every politician is aroused and at least verbally fighting pollution. With the close connection of population explosion and environmental abuse, even motherhood is being challenged.

Understanding the judicial trail of the conservation movement first requires a statement of the first lesson given to law school students in the basic civil procedure courses.

The right to relief in any civil action in any court consists of three elements. *First*, there must be a wrongful act, what lawyers call substantive wrong; torts, such as an act of assault, negligence, defamation or nuisance are examples, as are breaches of contract or of some other specific legal relationship. A rule of conduct, statutory or common law, must be broken by the defendant.

Second, the specific court must have jurisdiction of the subject matter of the suit and of the persons of the parties. No court has jurisdiction of all suits. Some are reserved for federal courts, some for state courts, some for tax courts and numerous other special courts. A person sued must be subject to the process of the court in which the suit is brought. This means that a defendant generally must be served in the state or other district in which the court lies.

Finally, there must be "standing" of the person suing. That is, the plaintiff must be one whom the court will deem a proper person to bring suit. In cases involving government acts or the acts of parties who were before administrative agencies before the matters came to court, the most frequently used term describing the person who has such standing is the "aggrieved party." He is the person injured or otherwise aggrieved by the action which he claims to be wrongful.

Where have conservationists stood, what has been the state of the law, with respect to these three elements?

The third element, that of standing, is clearly the area in which conservationists, operating through *ad hoc* citizens' committees or some of the established national and regional organizations, have made the most progress. They have probably won their battle for standing.

Basic rulings of the Supreme Court and other important courts, in environmental and other fields of law, have overruled older doctrines which required special personal injury to a person suing, which in the case of breach of duty by a public official meant injury beyond that suffered by the general public. Such older doctrines often had the ironic consequence of immunizing wrongdoing on a grand public scale, while granting relief from the comparatively minor wrongdoing of private persons resulting in damages as low as the proverbial six cents. The reapportionment cases are among the most important which have helped destroy the requirement of *special injury* to a plaintiff asserting a public right.

The foremost environmental case is the Storm King Mountain case, in which a federal court of appeals reversed the grant of a license, to New York City's Consolidated Edison Company, to build a power plant on Storm King Mountain. Against a background of centuries of the courts' major concern with pecuniary or property rights, there had been a growing series of exceptions to rules that one must be hurt in his pocketbook to be an aggrieved party. Therefore, the United States Court of Appeals for the Second Circuit held that the Scenic Hudson Preservation Conference, a citizen group with no pecuniary or property interest in the controversy, was a party "aggrieved" by the Federal Power Commission's grant of a license to build the plant at Storm King Mountain.

A number of cases in which the standing of conservationist and similar groups has been upheld have followed and broadened the rule of the "Scenic Hudson" case. Included are cases in which the Sierra Club is challenging a proposed Disneyland in Mineral King Canyon in California; in which a group of civil rights organizations challenged a superhighway across Nashville; and a complex of cases brought—by the Village of Tarrytown and an *ad hoc* citizens group together with what many call the "litigious" Sierra Club—to enjoin an expressway planned to be built in the Hudson River.

The standing hurdle, however, is only the first of the three that must be surmounted before the court rules that a river, forest or beach is to be left alone. The jurisdictional and substantive law problems remain.

The very classification of a question or problem as "jurisdictional" is often sufficient for most working lawyers and judges to leave the matter to the theoreticians and scholars who delight in finely spun theories often understood only by other theoreticians. Only a few of the jurisdictional problems of environmental cases can be briefly cited here. One such jurisdictional problem is that of "sovereign immunity," the theory that a sovereign nation or state or any agency of it is immune from suit, unless it consents to being sued. The rule is an application of the medieval and political axiom that the king (the sovereign) can do no wrong.

Many aspects of sovereign immunity have been done away with both by statutes and court decisions. Negligent operation of government vehicles is now almost as actionable as that of private vehicles. Federal and state courts of claims handle such suits. It is generally held that, if an act of a government agent is unconstitutional, he is not exempt from suit; he has no power to so act and, therefore, by one of the semantic tricks in which courts and lawyers specialize, the act is not that of the sovereign.

Still to be determined definitely, however, is the matter of whether an act of a government official which is illegal or beyond his statutory powers—but not necessarily beyond the powers which he could constitutionally be granted—is *ipso facto* not protected by the sovereign immunity doctrine. In many cases a distinction has been drawn between "discretionary" and "ministerial" acts in this connection. The government agent is immune from suit for any discretionary act.

The Hudson River Expressway case, in which the conservationists secured a trial court judgment enjoining the $200 million project involves fundamental sovereign immunity claims. The trial court held that the expressway is unlawful because construction of it necessarily involves "dike" and "causeway" structures which require Congressional consent under an 1899 law. It is conceded that no such consent was secured.

The government argues that even if the structures were correctly held to be dikes and causeways, and congressional consent were required, the federal officials granting the permit for such construction are immune from suit. They are the sovereign, it is said, and they have not waived immunity. The conservationists' answer is that law, if not order, is required of government officials as much as of trespassing students.

One other series of jurisdictional problems should be noted here, those of "federal jurisdiction." Most important conservation litigation has been and probably will continue to be brought in the federal courts. Where there is a choice of federal or state courts, conservationists will *generally* seek to go into the federal courts. They, it is felt, are less subject to the pressures of the financially interested groups in the immediate area of a project from which the local contractors, union members and merchants fancy they will grow rich.

Not every case, however, may be brought into a federal court. There must be federal jurisdiction for there to be a federal case. That jurisdiction is generally based upon the diversity of citizenship of the plaintiffs from that of the defendants, or the substantial involvement of federal questions, of rights or duties under federal laws. In diversity cases and in "federal question" cases, the problem of jurisdictional amount is often involved. Only if "the matter in controversy exceeds the sum or value of $10,000" is the jurisdictional amount present.

What is "the amount in controversy," however, when the very controversy is over rights and matters which are not measurable in dollars? Must the value of mountains or rivers or air be stated in dollars? If a dollar sign must be affixed to each "impulse from a vernal wood"—though it "teaches more of man, of moral evil and of good, than all the sages can"— conservationists must somehow fuse Wordsworth with Keynes and Friedman. And the fusion must be by a means permitted by Wigmore, the master scholar of the law and rules of evidence. So much for jurisdiction. The bulk of the problems are unresolved.

We turn to the third element, the substantive law. It is perhaps the most important, because all the standing and jurisdiction in the world is of no avail unless the defendant is breaching a rule of substantive law. In addition, if there is a clear breach, if conduct is clearly wrongful, a court will strain to sustain its jurisdiction to enjoin or punish such breach and to find that whoever is in court complaining has the standing to invoke that jurisdiction. The legal sword with which a plaintiff classically arms himself to pierce through the wrongdoer's procedural armor is the maxim that "wherever there is a wrong there is a remedy."

Environmentalists and their lawyers, through no fault of their own, have made little progress in the area of substantive law. In any particular proceedings the standing and jurisdictional battles are generally fought first, because the issues are posed by preliminary motions, involving no disputed facts, rather than by trial. Even more basic is the problem of changing vast bodies of substantive law which for centuries have been built around property or other pecuniary rights. The hearing of claims to aesthetic rights in and to lands, waters and air is still not the everyday practice of most courts.

Environmental lawyers and law teachers are hard at work trying to evolve, under present laws, theories of environmental rights *per se.* Some have promulgated theories based upon common law nuisance doctrines or the law of trusts. Serious study is being given to carving environmental rights out of the constitutional doctrines of "due process" and "equal protection."

While some successes may be achieved in courts by the use of such theories, environmentalists are battling steeply uphill. To prevail "on the merits" after sustaining their standing and the court's jurisdiction, they must continue to rely on finding illegality in the acts of the builders and polluters in some statute or rule not enacted or adopted with environmental rights in mind, or on a host of new anti-pollution and other resource protection statutes. The number and size of such statutes is expanding each month. The need remains for vast bodies of new laws that will reflect basic changes in our attitudes toward the limited resources of our one earth.

Shortly there may also be a dramatic upsurge in the demand for a constitutional grant of rights to a clean and livable environment. New York State has adopted a "conservation bill of rights." Senator Gaylord Nelson of Wisconsin, Congressman Richard Ottinger of New York and others are pushing such constitutional amendments.

The New York State constitutional amendment was originally incorporated in a proposed new state constitution adopted by the New York State Constitutional Convention of 1967. Because of serious Church v. State issues, the whole constitution was rejected by the voters in November, 1967. The Conservation Bill of Rights, however, was adopted by the Legislature and ratified by the voters of the state and became part of the state constitution in November, 1969. The basic policy declaration follows:

> The policy of the state shall be to conserve and protect its natural resources and scenic beauty and encourage the development and improvement of its agricultural lands for the production of food and other agricultural products. The legislature, in implementing this policy, shall include adequate provision for the abatement of air and water pollution and of excessive and unnecessary noise, the protection of agricultural lands, wetlands and shorelines, and the development and regulation of water resources. The legislature shall further provide for the acquisition of lands and waters, including improvements thereon and any interest therein, outside the forest preserve counties, and the dedication of properties so acquired or now owned, which because of their natural beauty, wilderness character, or geological, ecological or historical significance, shall be preserved and administered for the use and enjoyment of the people. Properties so dedicated shall constitute the state nature and historical preserve and they shall not be taken or otherwise disposed of except by law enacted by two successive regular sessions of the legislature.

A declaration of national policy almost as broad as the above is set forth in the "National Environmental Policy Act of 1969" which became law on January 1, 1970. This widely hailed legislation creates a Council on Environmental Quality and declares ". . . that it is the continuing policy of the Federal Government in cooperation with state and local governments and other serious public and private organizations to use all practicable means and measures . . . to create and maintain conditions under which man and nature can exist in productive harmony. . . ." The Act directs that "to the fullest extent possible . . . the policies, regulations and public laws of the United States shall be interpreted and administered in accordance with the policies set forth in this Act. . . ." It directs all agencies of the Federal Government to:

> . . . utilize a systematic, interdisciplinary approach which will insure the integrated use of the natural and social sciences and the environmental design arts in planning and in decisionmaking which may have an impact on man's environment.

Whether this national policy declaration affects immediately pending court actions and administrative proceedings—and gives rise to new rights which may be asserted in such actions and proceedings now being brought—is a question being studied by a number of environmental lawyers, scholars and law students. The particulars of the new body of common and statutory law which will reverse the processes of environmental degradation are not clear. It is certain, however, that the field has excited vast numbers of legal and judicial persons. And it can safely be said that a significant new body of law will develop out of such excitement.

Science and technology are the key to the future, the key to power, and the key to the solution of the problems we face today. They alone will not save us, but if we seek to untangle our problems without them, we are lost.

Chalmers Sherwin

In the last analysis, what will be scientifically available, politically acceptable, administratively feasible, economically justifiable, and morally tolerated depends on people's perceptions of consequences.

Bernard Berelson

Pollution Problems,
Resource Policy,
and the Scientist
Alfred W. Eipper

We know that man is degrading his natural environment, but we have no certain knowledge of how much or how fast. In this article I describe some of the salient characteristics of modern water pollution problems, and certain resource management principles that must be recognized in dealing with them. I then consider the implications of these problems and principles to the scientist's role in helping to maintain the quality of the environment.

POPULATION, TECHNOLOGY, AND WATER USE

The interacting effects of unchecked population growth and industrial and agricultural expansion cause most of our environmental problems. Man has taken some half million years to reach his present population, but he will double this within the next 40 years; the projected 100-million increase in the U.S. population over the next 30 years *(1)* can be represented as the addition of a new city of 270,000 inhabitants each month between now and A.D. 2000; four of our states now have population densities substantially higher than India's.

Demands on natural resources are increasing much faster than the population is. In the case of water, per capita use in the United States, exclusive of use for transportation and recreation, appears to be doubling every 40 years *(2)*. This means that in the 50 years it will take our population to double, *total* water use will quadruple. Hence the 1965 Department of Interior statement *(1)* that, under existing use patterns, the total amount of water needed just to sustain the present U.S. population for the remainder of their lives is greater than all the water that has been used by all people who have occupied the earth to date.

We tend to think of water supplies as fixed. In fact, however, increasing amounts of water are being rendered unusable through various forms of pollution. Although some uses do not make water unfit for certain purposes, our total usable water supplies are being reduced by pollution while demands for water accelerate sharply in response to the combined effects of population increase and technological development.

CASE STUDY

A recent—and still unsettled—controversy over pollution from a proposed power plant on Cayuga Lake, New York *(3)*, illustrates a type of pollution management problem that is becoming commonplace. After acquiring the plant site and conducting unpublicized preliminary surveys, the local electric utility company publicly announced its plans to construct an 830-megawatt nuclear-fueled steam turbine electric station next to its small coal-fired plant already operating on the lake. Cayuga Lake has a mean flushing time of 9 years and remains thermally stratified for about 6 months of the year. In the company plan, water at 45°F (7.2C°) for cooling the nuclear plant's condensers would be obtained from a depth of about 100 feet (30 meters) in the hypolimnion (the cold bottom layer), warmed 20° to 25°F, and returned to the epilimnion (the warmer top layer) at a rate of 1100 cubic feet (30.8 cubic meters) per second (500,000 gallons per minute), year-round.

A number of scientists in the area (many of them, but not all, biologists) were concerned about the predictable and the possible ill effects of this operation on the lake. Some of the predictable results would be to increase the volume of the epilimnion, enrich it with nutrients removed from the hypolimnion, and prolong the stratification period, and hence lengthen the "growing season" in the surface waters. Secondary effects such as changes in species composition or numerical relationships in the lake's plant and animal populations, further oxygen depletion in the bottom waters in summer, and increased heat storage in winter were additional possibilities. Small quantities of radionuclides discharged into the condenser cooling water would become concentrated in this slow-flushing lake, and further concentrations could be expected biologically through food chains and physically through local irregularities in water circulation patterns. The concerned scientists based their estimates of the possible magnitudes of these effects on models which they felt utilized the fewest and simplest valid assumptions, coupled with scattered limnological data on Cayuga Lake accumulated over the past 50 years.

Other individuals and groups in the local scientific community arrived at various other estimates—many of them less severe—of the nature and magnitude of the power plant's possible effects on the lake, using different models, assumptions, and interpretations of past data. Few of the individuals or groups, however, seem to have been concerned with seriously challenging the validity of estimates put forward by others. In retrospect, it appears that more critical comparison and discussion of these different views by their proponents would have been productive.

A particularly encouraging by-product of this controversy was a great deal of imaginative thinking on the problem by a wide variety of scientists, engineers, economists, and others. It is this kind of thinking that will ultimately provide significant solutions to pollution problems. One physicist, for example, suggested using some of the generated electricity to remove nutrients from the water in its passage through the cooling cycle, thus reducing the lake's present rate of eutrophication (aging). Other scientists proposed an ingenious scheme for building a pumped-storage cooling pond on the plain several hundred feet above the lakeshore plant site. Company spokesmen said this scheme was not economically feasible; their critics replied that the company's assessment of the plan was prejudiced and superficial.

Perhaps the simplest method for reducing the possibilities of thermal damage to Cayuga Lake from the proposed plant would be to take the cooling water from the lake's upper layer (above a depth of 40 feet) and return it to the surface. This would be equivalent to operating the plant on a river, estuary, or any other unstratified body of water where the temperature of the intake water varies seasonally. It might require only the use of low-profile, mechanical draft cooling units during about 4 months of the year.

The utility company's actions in the Cayuga Lake case seem to illustrate a behavior pattern fairly common in controversies of this general type. The strategy was to announce the proposal *after* plans for implementing it were already well under way, and to keep things moving ahead rapidly thereafter. The substance of the company's numerous publicity releases was that the plant would benefit the community in many ways, and that the company would never allow the plant to "harm" the lake, and was conducting contract research projects which, it said, were expected to demonstrate that its operations would not damage the lake *(4)*. That the company did indeed contract with highly qualified independent research teams to make at least two studies is to its credit. (Needless to say, the researchers did not share the company's preconception of what the results might show.) Critics of the company were frankly skeptical of the value of a 1-year research project, in view of the enormous complexity of a large lake ecosystem and the great annual (and other) variations in data already obtained from Cayuga and similar environments.

Company spokesmen tended to be closemouthed, unwilling to debate issues or to discuss alternatives, and generally confined themselves to rather standardized publicity releases and announcements. They were challenged on their lack of receptiveness to the idea of using already available technological safeguards that would eliminate virtually all hazard of thermal and radiological pollution to Cayuga Lake—technology whose cost could be passed on to consumers and would add less than 25 cents a month to the electricity bill of the average household, according to calculations from company data. Company officials, although obviously reluctant to consider adding the safeguards to the plant's proposed design, were equally unwilling to discuss in concrete, meaningful terms, the reasons for their reluctance (5). Their public posture still seems to be that the only feasible way to operate the plant is by the relatively unique method that they have proposed from the outset.

The company proved to have been less than frank in some instances, and indeed appeared cynical. For example, it developed that the company had already (i) invested some $5 million or more in site preparation and (ii) contracted to sell half to three-fourths of its power to Consolidated Edison, in New York City (6), while research to assure that the lake would not be harmed was under way and before even 1 year's data were available for analysis.

Byron Saunders (7) summarizes the Cayuga Lake case as follows.

> Oversimplifying the case, then, the position of one group is that because facts are not at hand, the design of the station should be such that all precautions be taken to guarantee as much cooling as necessary so the lake will not be affected in any detrimental way. The position of the company is that to provide for the maximum possible protection would be too costly and unjustified, because absolute knowledge that it would be necessary is not available. I might point out that this is a regulated industry and that any legitimate capital costs that are necessary for generation facilities are proper elements for the rate base, and hence the company's concern cannot be the ability to recover the costs involved. The real reasons appear to me to be political, and the ability of the private utility to compete with comparable rates of some of the public or quasi-public utilities that are reaching into

this area. What this example seems to represent is the much too prevalent case of concentrating one's interest and attention on the cost of the primary product or service with insufficient concern for the side effects that the minimum cost concept generally produces.

An active, well-organized, and growing citizens' group concerned with possible effects of the proposed power plant was formed about a year after the utility's first public announcement of its construction plans. Activities of this group, and of others concerned, induced regional political representatives to initiate public hearings on the issue before various state legislative bodies. Subsequently those legislators most directly involved introduced three bills which provided effective and reasonable safeguards against thermal and radionuclide pollution of lakes—in particular, by power plants. Two of these bills were passed virtually unanimously by both arms of the state legislature, but the Governor subsequently vetoed them. The third bill passed the Assembly unanimously, but eventually was killed in Senate committee.

By November 1969 reports from both of the short-term utility-sponsored research projects on Cayuga Lake had been published. It appears that the company will now proceed to apply for a state permit to operate the power plant without cooling devices, and the local Citizens' Committee is girding for another hearing.

POLLUTION PROBLEMS IN GENERAL

Perhaps the most obvious feature of pollution problems is that new ones are proliferating—in complexity as well as kind—faster than we are able to understand and solve them. Answers seem to accrue at arithmetic rates; pollution problems, at geometric rates.

Two other characteristics of pollution problems are their unpredictability and their persistence. Repeatedly we have proved unable to foresee either the intensity or the scope of pollution effects before they emerge as some form or forms of serious environmental degradation. Also, we are learning from harsh experience that many of these unforeseen effects are largely irreversible, at least within the time span of a human life. Thus, within the past few years we have come to realize that, in the earth's atmosphere, nitrogen oxides, particulate matter, lead, radionuclides, carbon dioxide, and perhaps also heat have increased, and in most cases these increases are continuing. DDT is now distributed throughout soils, waters, and people throughout the world, and it even appears in the body fat of antarctic penguins. It and other durable toxic pesticides have virtually ended reproduction of valuable fishes in bodies of water such as Lake George, New York, possibly for many years to come *(8)*. Each of these is an unanticipated pollution problem for which there is no immediate cure.

Causal relationships between pollutants and environmental degradation are usually much harder to demonstrate than was the case for Lake George. Because all natural systems are highly complex, we cannot quickly or clearly prove even extensive long-term damage to such a system, any more than we can conclusively prove (to the manufacturers' satisfaction) that cigarette smoking is injurious to health. Damage from pollution can seldom, if ever, be predicted with certainty, and, if it can be proved after it has occurred, the proof is likely to be too late, as in the case of Lake Erie.

TYPICAL ATTITUDES OF POLLUTERS

A constructive approach to pollution problems requires more than knowledge of pollution results; we also need to understand the human motives and actions that produce them. Often development plans involve serious threats to water quality and aquatic environments through introductions of heat, radionuclides, nutrients such as phosphorus and nitrogen, toxic chemicals, silt, decomposing organic matter, and so on.

The special-interest groups promoting such developments may be industries that wish to use the water or other resource in a way that will yield them maximum profit, or they may be persons whose welfare or sympathies are more indirectly tied to an industry's success. The latter category includes groups of citizenry primarily concerned with immediate industrial benefits to the local economy, and persons in state or federal agencies who are much concerned with promoting the development of industrial technology. (Unfortunately, many of these agencies are assigned the dual role of promoting *and* regulating an industry.) Technological interest groups often make irrational assertions (based on questionable assumptions) to support programs that will exploit public natural resources. These assertions—or implications—include the following.

The program—as proposed—*has* to be enacted *now.*

The program will be enacted in any event. You can't stop progress.

The program is needed to fill the demand that will be created by the program.

No one opposes the program. It will benefit the majority, and harm no one.

Data used to estimate effects of the program are the only valid, pertinent data available.

Since there is no proof that the development will damage the environment, we can safely assume it will not.

All effects of the program have been considered.

The program, as presented, represents the sum total of the development contemplated for this particular resource.

All applicable alternatives have been considered.

Not only should such assumptions be questioned when they appear in discussions of pollution issues, but other questions should be asked, such as the following.

Who participated in formulating the assumptions and conclusions about this program's desirability?

What lasting social benefits—and costs—will this program produce? Who will derive these benefits?

What environmental problems will, or may, be created?

What alternatives exist? Has the relative desirability of not enacting the program been evaluated?

RESOURCE MANAGEMENT PRINCIPLES

In light of the ecological, technological, and human aspects of pollution, we can identify certain resource management principles that apply particularly to problems of pollution control.

> 1. Because almost any decision on management of a natural resource involves the allocation of an essentially fixed (or diminishing) resource among a growing number of competing and expanding uses, it is appropriate to ask first, Who makes such a decision? I believe there is growing evidence and awareness that these decisions must be basically public decisions and cannot be made unilaterally by any particular interest group, be it industrialist or preservationist. One reason for this is that the resources involved are public resources. They concern quality of the environment—quality of life— for all users. Another reason is that there is an increasing number of widely differing, and often competing, demands on the same resource. Cayuga Lake, for example, is used extensively for boating, water supply (municipal, agricultural, domestic, and industrial), fishing, electric power generation, swimming, residence, flood control, water skiing, waste disposal, camping, hunting, and so on.
>
> 2. Narrow, "conventional" economic criteria are at best inadequate and at worst disastrously mislead- ing if used as the sole basis for decisions about

natural resources. In deciding what criteria to employ for estimating values and determining priorities in the uses of a natural resource, the governing principle should be to include the widest possible variety of applicable criteria and, above all, to avoid resorting to a single criterion. Resource economists are often the first to point out the severe limitations of dollar values as the only basis for weighing (or justifying) all elements in an allocation complex. As stated by a committee of the Congress *(9)*:

The market approach fails for two reasons: First, it is very difficult to quantify in dollar terms many of the values of environmental quality. Second, the axiom that a unit of profit is more valuable now than at any time in the future leads to short-sightedness in environmental management.

There are other quantitative measures of environmental value that often should be used to supplement dollar criteria, such as priority ranks and environmental diversity indices *(10)*. A decision on a public resource must also take into consideration, through hearings and other media, those wishes of, and values to, the users that can be expressed only through the political process. In the final analysis, decisions on the management of a natural resource are basically political decisions.

3. Another resource management principle involves communication and candor. Impending environmental problems must be promptly recognized and widely discussed as soon as they are perceived. A satisfactory resolution of a conflict over resources can be obtained only when all parties communicate openly, honestly, and freely from the outset, and recognize that the ultimate solution to such a conflict may well be a compromise. If, for example,

the Cayuga Lake power plant could be built and operated, but with safeguards to the lake's ecology that would not substantially increase the cost of electricity, this obviously would be an unusually good compromise. But satisfactory compromises, difficult to achieve at best, are even more difficult to achieve without free and open communication. The kind of communication that seems to typify resource management controversies today is generally a communication between adversaries. Regulatory agencies must give sincere, serious consideration to the concerns of citizens about environmental hazards from a technology. Failure of such agencies to require that available safeguards be used may force the citizenry into outright opposition to the technology.

4. We cannot disregard impending pollution problems in the belief that science and technology will correct any maladjustments that might subsequently appear in an ecosystem. "Pollution control regulations" that permit discharge of a pollutant, with the stipulation that the polluter must be prepared to correct pollution later (should this "prove" necessary), are usually based on wishful thinking about the availability of proof at some future date.

5. We have an obligation to future generations to maintain the quality of the natural environment. Everyone has a right to a high-quality environment; no one user has a right to pollute without the consent of other users. The burden of proof must be on the potential polluter to demonstrate that he will not pollute, rather than on the public to prove that pollution has occurred.

6. Closely linked to this is the principle that all of us must pay for what we use, whether the use be recreation, sewage disposal, or consumption of electricity, coal, or water. As stressed by Saunders *(7)*, "Let those who dance pay the fiddler. If in our affluent society, we cannot pay the full cost of the products and services we want, do we have the right to expect future generations to pay for our indulgences?" A recent Gallup poll *(11)* showed that about three-fourths of the total sample from the U.S. population were deeply concerned about the quality of the environment and willing to pay additional taxes to maintain it. Lessons from past mistakes indicate that repair of the environment, even when possible, can seldom be justified economically. Industries should concentrate their expenditures for research and development on (i) devising new technology that will keep conflicts with other resource uses to a minimum, and (ii) helping finance the assessment of new technology before proliferating it.

7. When planning a program that involves exploitation of a natural resource, we must give equal consideration to *each* of the possible means of achieving the program objective, or objectives, using "possible" in the broadest context and including consideration of all possible locations for the program. Electric utilities and their promoters cite the fact that needs for electricity are doubling every 10 years or less, and they protest that conservation groups block them at every turn. Usually, however, the only sites and operating methods considered feasible by power companies are those which are "economical" in a very narrow sense, as in the Cayuga Lake case.

8. The principle of sustained yield, familiar to resource managers as a harvesting concept, has wider applications of growing importance to today's environmental problems. This principle is stated succinctly in "Managing the Environment" *(9)*:

The use of the environment is a necessary and acceptable concept. The difference is that future use must be in the recycle context of perpetual renewal and reuse, not the old pattern of use and discard. A sort of stable state between civilization and the environment is called for—not a balance of nature (for nature is always changing in its own right) but a harmony of society and the environment within natural laws of physics, chemistry, and biology.

9. Last but far from least, we must employ the principle of prevention. As mentioned above, man's adverse influences on natural environments are accelerating and becoming increasingly complex. There is now abundant evidence of severe limitations on our ability to predict, prove, or reverse pollution effects. For these reasons, waiting to measure environmental damage from a technology before taking steps to correct it is no longer a tenable approach. We must place more emphasis on using whatever knowledge is already available to recognize and interpret threats to the environment before they become realities, and must be willing to act on the premise that, when the likelihood of damage can be foreseen, the damage should be forestalled. It is far easier to prevent pollution (or nuclear warfare, or overpopulation) than to correct for it after it has occurred. We should realize that there is at least as much need for safety factors in managing our natural environment as there is in planning a bridge or a boiler. The trial-and-error method is a dangerous one when applied to environmental management. As Senator

Edmund Muskie has said of thermal pollution of water *(12)*: "You've got to take the point of view that if we don't know enough, we don't know enough to permit the discharge."

THE SCIENTIST'S ROLE

Global ecologists point out that our planet is in fact a space vehicle with a mushrooming human population and a balanced, continuously recycling life-support system. Because key elements of this system are increasingly threatened by man's pollution activities, we must develop an effective early-warning process. Scientists must be willing to involve themselves in this process by detecting and publicizing foreseeable threats to the environment *(13)*. This is not to suggest any lessened importance of long-term research on the causes and effects of pollution. Our focus here is simply on another dimension of pollution: those impending problems which require preventive action now.

What are some of the functions required of the scientist in this early-warning approach to a potential pollution situation? First, this approach involves ferreting out and analyzing all pertinent data that are available *now*. Frank Di Luzio, former Assistant Secretary of the Interior for Water Pollution Control, stated the concept well *(14)*:

> . . . all of us would like to know all the facts about the problems we are dealing with. Since we never will know all the facts, we've got to do the best we can with the facts at hand. To a considerable extent we must forego the satisfaction of dealing with incontrovertible scientific data and be guided simply by prima facie evidence.

Next, the scientist must be willing to publicize his tentative conclusions from the data, and his assessment of alternative management measures and the likely effects of each which these conclusions suggest to him. It is not enough to "let the facts speak for themselves." The scientist, as a trained and experienced specialist, has an obligation to give society his professional interpretation of those facts. It is also essential to the validity of the decision-making process that he identify this as *his*—not *the*—interpretation. When scientists disagree in their interpretations, they should discuss and analyze the sources of disagreement, for the ultimate benefit of society.

I suspect a majority of scientists are disquieted by at least some aspects of the role outlined above. It stipulates the unpleasant necessity of going out on a shaky limb of tentative conclusions. It often involves a kind of limelight the scientist would rather avoid, and it may involve him, at least peripherally, in unaccustomed controversy. Nevertheless the scientist must face the fact that he is now living in a different ecosystem, with critical new problems, on a new time scale, that require new approaches. Only the dedicated scientific recluse can totally ignore these new responsibilities. The early-warning approach requires that scientists call the shots as they see them and remember that debate is central to scientific progress. They should recognize that straddling a fence too long can produce sterility, and that when one has reached the point of making all his communications noncontroversial there is no further need for him to communicate.

The role of the scientist, as such, should not extend beyond presentation and defense of his estimate of pollution hazards and an assessment of alternatives. He has an obligation to make available information from his profession that will help the voter make a more enlightened decision, but he must scrupulously avoid telling him how to vote. Because decisions on environmental management are so complex, they must represent the best possible reconciliation of many different interests; hence they must be public decisions. The scientist can contribute much to the *basis* for a public decision, but in *making* that decision he has only one vote. He is no more entitled—and no more qualified—than any other citizen to elect which of various alternative courses should be followed.

On the other hand he is no *less* entitled or qualified to choose. The scientist should not, from fear that his professional identity will give him unfair advantage, shrink from exercising the political rights of a private citizen to express his personal views (so identified) on a controversial issue. Although quite properly concerned about his credibility as a scientist, he should not disregard his credibility as a human being and voter with genuine convictions.

SUMMARY

Through exponential increase in population, accompanied by rapid industrial and agricultural expansion, we have reached the point where decisions involving the use of natural resources are much more important and also much more difficult than they were even 10 years ago. The same conditions that make decisions more urgent make them more time-consuming. The Cayuga Lake case illustrates many aspects of a present-day resource management controversy.

Because we are being forced to make increasingly critical decisions about ecosystems for which reliable predictive data are often lacking, we must, collectively, develop a framework of genuinely useful principles to guide our dealings with natural environments. I have suggested a few such principles, and the scientist's role in implementing them.

REFERENCES AND NOTES

1. "Quest for Quality," *U.S. Dep. Interior Conserv. Yearb.* (1965), p. 10.
2. "The Nation's Water Resources," *U.S. Water Resources Council Publ.* (1968), p. 4.
3. Accounts of this controversy have appeared in various publications, including the following: A. W. Eipper *et al.*, *Thermal Pollution of Cayuga Lake by a Proposed Power Plant* (Authors, 1968); C. A. Carlson *et al.*, *Radioactivity and a Proposed Power Plant on Cayuga Lake* (Authors, Cornell Univ., Ithaca, 1968); L. J. Carter, *Science* 1962, 649 (1968); J. Hampton, *Nat. Observ.* 8, No. 5, 1 (1969).
4. "Bell Station Preliminary Safety Analysis Report," *N.Y. State Elec. Gas Corp. Publ.* (1968), pp. II-4-4, 6, 11.

5.   One of the difficulties sometimes associated with such cases is the fact that a utility may fear that the public service regulatory body will not permit a raise in rates that would make it possible to pass on the costs of environmental protection to the consumer. There seems to be no public information on whether such corporate apprehension existed—or was justified—in the Cayuga Lake case.

6.   *Nucleonics Week* 1969, 4 (16 Jan. 1969).

7.   B. W. Saunders, *J. Eng. Educ.*, in press.

8.   G. E. Burdick, E. J. Harris, H. J. Dean, T. M. Walker, J. Skea, D. Colby, *Trans. Amer. Fish. Soc.* 93, 127 (1964).

9.   "Managing the Environment," *Publ. Comm. Sci. Astronaut, 90th Congr., 2nd Session*, 1968 (Government Printing Office, Washington, D.C., 1968), pp. 14-15.

10. A. W. Eipper, F. W. Howell, R. J. Kalter, R. L. Shelton, B. T. Wilkins, "Aspects of Planning, Evaluation, and Decision-Making in Sport Fishery Management," *Cornell Univ. Conserv. Dept. Publ.* (1970).

11. *Nat. Wildlife* 7, No. 3, 18 (1969).

12. Quoted in *New York Times* 1969, 12E (9 Mar. 1969).

13. It is encouraging to note the growing recognition of this necessity by scientists such as R. S. Morison [*Science* 165, 150 (1969)] and O. M. Solandt [*ibid.*, p. 445].

14. Quoted in "A New Era for America's Waters," *Fed. Water Pollut. Contr. Admin. Publ.* (1967).

15. This article is adapted from a paper presented in August 1969 at the Engineering Foundation Research Conference on Technology Assessment, Andover, N.H. I thank the many colleagues who critically reviewed the manuscript.

We must have a new industrial revolution even if a few of us have to generate it. Other industrial revolutions have come about unplanned. The first was hailed as a way of ennobling human beings by substituting steam and electrical power for their muscles. This it undoubtedly did, but the generation of power brought with it side effects—including air pollution—which, far from being ennobling, were and continue to be degrading to human existence. In the second revolution the multiplication of "things" came about—"things" that at last could be mass-produced, so that people could have more and more of them. Thus was generated the solid-waste problem.

A third revolution was the tremendous growth in industrial chemistry, and the ability to tailor-make chemicals in vast quantities very cheaply, for all kinds of purposes—for example, pesticides intended to selectively destroy forms of life inimical to various groups of human beings. But these turned out not to be so selective; they have upset the little-understood ecological balance, and have polluted and poisoned the waters.

In preparation for the next industrial revolution, I suggest that we revise our vocabulary. For instance, there is no such thing, no such person, as a consumer. We merely *use* "things"; and, according to the law of the conservation of matter, exactly the same mass of material is discarded after use. Thus, as the standard of living goes up, the amount of waste and consequent pollution must go up.

I believe we must base the next industrial revolution—a planned one—on the thesis that there is no such thing as waste, that waste is simply some useful substance that we do not yet have the wit to use. Industry so far is doing only half its job. It performs magnificent feats of scientific, technological, and managerial skill to take things from the land, refine them, and mass-manufacture, mass-market, and mass-distribute them to the so-called consumer; then the same mass of material is left, after use, to the so-called public sector, to be "disposed of." By and large, in our society, the private sector makes the things *before* use and the public sector disposes of them *after* use.

In the next industrial revolution, there must be a loop back from the user to the factory, which industry must close. If American industrial genius can mass-assemble and mass-distribute, why cannot the same genius mass-collect, mass-disassemble, and massively reuse the materials? If American industry should take upon itself the task of closing this loop, then its original design of the articles would include features facilitating their return and remaking. If, on the other hand, we continue to have the private sector make things and the public sector dispose of them, designs for reuse will not easily come about.

We industrial revolutionaries must plan to move more and more into the fields of human service, and not leave such concerns to the so-called public sector. We have seen our food supply grow to abundance in the United States, with fewer and fewer people needed to grow it. We are seeing the automation of factories, with an abundance of "things" provided by fewer and fewer people. On the other hand, we have a shortage of human services and a shortage of people providing these services. It follows quite simply that, if private enterprise is not to dwindle, while the public sector grows to be an all-embracing octopus, then private enterprise must go into the fields of human service.

The next industrial revolution is on our doorstep. Let us be the revolutionaries who shape it, rather than have it happen—and shape us.

Athelstan Spilhaus

The Experimental City
Athelstan Spilhaus

The Experimental City suggested some years ago is now being planned. Started from scratch, the Experimental City will be unlike other cities or towns that have been built in this way. It will not be a bedroom satellite of an existing city, as some of the New Towns in England have become; nor will it attempt to be an instant utopia. It will be neither a single company town—Hershey, Pennsylvania—nor a single occupation town—Oak Ridge, Manned Space Center, Los Alamos, Chandrigar, Brazilia, Washington, D.C. The Experimental City should not be confused with "demonstration" or "model" cities that attempt to show what can be done temporarily to renew old cities. Yet it will experiment with extensions of many of the assets and experiences of these. It will attempt to be a city representing a true cross section of people, income, business and industry, recreation, education, health care, and cultural opportunities that are representative of the United States.

The Experimental City will be carefully planned for the specific purpose of people's living and working, but, like a machine, it will be planned for an optimum population size. When it reaches this capacity, its growth will be stopped, just as machines are not overloaded when they reach their capacity. Even bacterial cultures stop growing when their size is such that they can no longer get rid of their waste metabolites. Man has not only the products of his own metabolism but what James Lodge calls the metabolites of his labor-saving slaves. Buckminster Fuller estimates that each of us has the equivalent of four hundred slaves. As technology proceeds, more and more of these mechanical slaves are used. In turn, waste metabolites increase, and cities should decrease proportionally in size.

For the experiment to be real, the city must be large enough to offer a variety of job opportunities and recreational, educational, and cultural choices. Fortunately, as technology moves forward, it affords a variety of choices without needing great numbers of people. For example, television can bring to a small community a variety in education, recreation, and information that in the past would have been possible only in large urban areas.

Three million people—the annual population increase in the United States—is equivalent to a dozen cities of 250,000 people. No engineer nor industry would build a dozen of anything so costly and complicated as a city without having an experimental prototype. The three million new citizens must be housed anyway, and the experience of many industries tells us that it is often cheaper to build a new modern plant than to patch an old one. To allow our presently overgrown cities, burdened as they are with complex problems, to take care of an unplanned bulge is costly.

Cities grow unplanned; they just spread haphazardly. By planning now, the advantages of high-density living can be preserved without the ugliness, filth, congestion, and noise that presently accompany city living. The urban mess is due to unplanned growth—too many students for the schools, too much sludge for the sewers, too many cars for the highways, too many sick for the hospitals, too much crime for the police, too many commuters for the transport system, too many fumes for the atmosphere to bear, too many chemicals for the water to carry.

The immediate threat must be met as we would meet the threat of war—by the mobilization of people, industry, and government. The potential gains are so great that we should take correspondingly calculated experimental risks. Curiously, we only take great risks and tolerate great mistakes in war. Up to now, government's efforts have been ineffective, concentrating on measuring what is happening, then viewing with alarm, and making industry the scapegoat in what are often essentially punitive measures. Instead, government should provide incentives to industry to encourage control of waste at its source.

Imaginative things are being done to control waste at its source. Fly ash from smokestacks is collected for use in making cement and bricks, but, so far only one sixteenth of the total has a market; a plant in Florida uses a city's garbage to make fertilizer; dust from grain elevators is made into pellets for cattle feed; iron-ore dust from steel plants is fed back to make steel; sulfur dioxide from factory chimneys and sulfur from oil refineries is made into sulfuric acid. There are examples of industrial symbiosis where one industry feeds off, or at least neutralizes, the wastes of another—inorganic wastes from a chemical plant may neutralize the over-abundance of organic nutrients from sewage and prevent uncontrollable growth of algae.

In many of these cases, the cost of recovery far exceeds the value of the recovered material. But if a clean environment is our aim, it costs the nation less to recover wastes where they are generated, even if they have no value, than to clean them up after they have been dispersed. Costs resultant from control at the source must be passed on in the cost of the product, but the total increase in manufacturing costs would not compare to the amount the nation would have to spend for cleaning up after the filth is dispersed in rivers, in the air, or on the land.

But what about the manufactured goods themselves once they are in the consumer's hands? We call him a consumer, but he consumes nothing. Eventually he must discard the same mass of material that he uses. Just as the iron-ore dust is recycled into the steel mill, manufactured hardware articles must be recycled after use. This process would close the loop from manufacture, to user, back to the factory. Total recycling is the ultimate goal, for it would eliminate waste and pollution. The automobile, for example, should be designed at the start with its eventual reclamation in mind. The automobile industry serves the public magnificently by mass-producing, mass-marketing, and mass-distributing a highly complex and useful machine. The industry could equally well apply its imagination and use its farflung network of operations to collect, disassemble, and reuse used cars.

In recycling, the *consumer* becomes a *user* which he has, in fact, always been. He essentially "rents" everything. If the automobile were designed with reclamation in mind, the widespread distribution network could double as the collection network. The same applies to refrigerators, washing machines, vacuum cleaners, and every piece of hardware that we use and throw away via the euphemistic "trade-in" process. Complete recycling makes "trade-in" real and meaningful.

In the water-pollution problem, recycling—the multiple use of water of different qualities—is the ultimate goal. We never use up any water; it just carries nutrients and flushes wastes and heat from our systems. One simple example is a totally enclosed greenhouse in the desert. Water with dissolved plant foods flows into hydroponic gardens, is transpired by the plants in the hot part of the greenhouse, sucked to a cooled part where it recondenses and acquires more dissolved nutrients to repeat the cycle. The only water needed is a cupful now and then to offset leakage.

The emotional prophets of doom and the sanitary engineers provide us with a dismal picture of how fast we must run using conventional methods merely to prevent the situation from getting worse. We commend Los Angeles for taking a legislative step toward controlling the automobile emissions that cause smog, but if they achieve this control of the unburned hydrocarbons, they will blissfully go on, the automobiles will increase, and by 1980 the oxides of nitrogen, an inevitable result of burning air with anything, may reach dangerous proportions.

We need total recycling, control at the source, symbiosis of industry, and experiments with entirely new technologies toward this end. Often new technologies cannot be tried in the older cities because they are incompatible with existing systems and obsolete legal, labor, and taxation codes. The new subway in New York is not new; it is merely an extension of the old.

Some economists maintain that total recycling is too expensive, but neither they nor anyone else knows the staggering cost of present waste mismanagement. Other economists, with commendable confidence in the abilities of scientists and engineers, say "why worry to recycle"—we can invent substitutes for anything we may run out of. But recycling conserves not only what we ordinarily think of as natural resources, but also the one God-given resource that we cannot reinvent once we destroy it—our natural environment.

To preserve the total quality of the natural environment, we must think of pollution in a broad sense. Pollution would then embrace all the ills of a city. Using *disease* as an antonym of *ease*, Dr. R. K. Cannan has spoken of a different kind of disease from environmental pollution. In this context, "disease" embraces the psychological insult to aesthetic sensitivity that even a perfectly sanitized junk yard presents. Filthy environments may make us mentally ill before they make us physically sick.

A pollutant often neglected is noise. Environmental noise in cities is rapidly reaching levels that industry has long considered harmful to the ears. Even lower levels of the continuously irritating noises of a concentrated civilization may make serious contributions to mental sickness. Noise is a product of the cities: Jet airplanes land near cities, trucks bring goods into cities, machines are concentrated in cities, and noisy pavement breakers are always digging up city streets. Cutting down noise costs money too; silencing a jet engine reduces its power, and a quiet machine is usually overpowered.

People concentrate in cities to escape the rigors of climate and to maximize social, business, and cultural contacts with others with a minimum of travel. But when cities grow too large, the urban climate deteriorates to such an extent that people flee. Like the nomadic peoples of primitive times who moved with the seasons, they travel far to live in the uneasy compromise of suburbia. In the summer, the power stations of the cities exude waste heat, the buildings prevent breezes from carrying off fumes and heat, and air conditioning pumps heat from the buildings to the streets to aggravate the situation further.

We need a mathematical computer model study of where waste should be taken, where it could do the most good in the insulating belt around the city. We should plan our cities on the basis of maps of pollution proneness. The industrialization of Appalachia with dirty industry is ridiculous. Those mountains were called the Smokies by the first men who saw them because they were so prone to pollution due to stagnant anticyclones that even the natural turpentines hung in a haze.

Pollution comes from concentration: Half our national population crowds onto 1 per cent of the land. People flock to the cities because they like high-density living. Fortunately, high-density living can give better and cheaper public service. It is a well-known axiom that the bigger the lots, the lower the caliber of public service. High-density living *per se* has not caused the filth in the cities; the assemblages have simply grown too large. If the one hundred million people that represent half the population of the U.S. today lived in the same high density as they do now, but were dispersed in eight hundred smaller concentrations of one-quarter million apiece, there would probably be no serious pollution problem. We need urban *dispersal,* not urban renewal.

Politicians are now stressing the need for industry and the private sector to take part in the rebuilding of slums in old, overgrown cities. Why should they? What bank would make a long-term loan to rebuild a slum in a city so overgrown that it would be a slum again before the mortgage was paid off? Moreover, what good would it do for people in the long run? Part of the problem is that our elected officials, particularly since reapportionment, represent districts. Politicians are most numerous where the population is most dense. There is little incentive for an elected official to suggest dispersal of his own thickly populated and easily covered district. Consequently, we hear little of urban dispersal, but a good deal about renewal, which usually means going faster the wrong way and bringing more people into already overcrowded precincts.

Such considerations led me to urge the Experimental City project. This will provide a laboratory for experimentation and a prototype for future dispersed systems with separated cities of high concentration and controlled size. As yet, no one has studied what the best size for a city is, nor attempted to keep a city to a certain size. Chambers of Commerce uniformly believe that bigger is better. We must get away from this conventional thinking and realize that bigger than an undetermined optimum size is not better.

A city of one hundred thousand may be too small for the diversity of cultural, recreational, educational, health-care, and work opportunities that make for a virile self-contained community. Eight or ten million has, however, been amply proved to be too big. Somewhere in between lies an optimum number.

Once we have decided on a city's optimum size, how do we prevent the uncontrolled growth that leads to many of today's urban problems? The answer is *not* to control individuals, but to design a mix of industrial, commercial, and other employment opportunities that keeps the population in a healthy equilibrium. In the absence of better information on the proportion in a healthy mix, perhaps we should start with a cross section of the United States. But what about regional differences? A healthy mix in the Northwest might be quite different from the comfortable mix in the Southeast. Social scientists have a challenge to define these mixes. The whole concept behind the Experimental City begins and ends with people. Profiles of employees in various enterprises can be studied by wage level, group preferences, and any other factors important to a healthy representative sample, including the right quota of those dependent on welfare, the very young, and the old and retired. Here again, regional differences of employee preferences must be considered in relation to the industrial mix.

A city grows because business and industry concentrate there, providing people with diverse opportunities for work and a variety of life styles. If an Experimental City is to be built to preserve a better quality of urban environment, industry and business must build it, but in a planned way.

Although the Experimental City would be planned as much as possible, it would be designed and built so that it could change easily. In a way, the city would be designed backwards, starting with innovations in the newest engineering systems conceived for a certain number of people and no more. It would be designed to remove the burdens of chores and filth, which modern technology can do. It goes without saying that one designs for man and his society and, in general, the planning of transportation, communication, feeding, and other networks comes later. In this case, one would use technological innovation to reduce physical restraints, which would hopefully allow man and his society more freedom to thrive. The crux is to remove the pollutants of chores, filth, noise, and congestion from the city in the hope that this will free the city dweller for a greater choice and diversity of individual human activities.

People congregate in the city because it is a gathering place for work and social interaction. Thus, working and living must be compatible, but often the factories for work make the environment for living unpleasant or unbearable. Clearly the most dramatic role of industry in the Experimental City is to show that places of work need not pollute the environment with congestion, fumes, dirty water, and noise. If living and working conditions are compatible, then people will not have to travel so much. Because of pollutants, cities are divided into separate residential and industrial areas. With the pollutants removed, industrial, commercial, residential, and educational institutions could exist side by side, reducing the human waste of commuting to and fro. If the technology of the Experimental City succeeds, there will be no need for zoning. In the interim, we should recognize four-dimensional zoning which adds a time dimension to space zoning. An example of this is the control of noise at airports, where planes are prevented from taking off during the night.

Improved communications also reduce the need for travel. As a start, an information utility could be devised that would link by broad-band coaxial cables all points now connected by telephone wires. The information utility, possibly with two-way, point-to-point video and other broad-band communication, would remove much of the obvious waste in the present conduct of business and commerce, banking and shopping. (Housewives would have bedside shopping and banking, and tele-baby-sitting when they went to visit a neighbor.) City-wide improved communications with access to the central hospital open up the possibility of less costly, less intense services and better, more abundant home care. These, of course, are not radical ideas—but extensions. (Pediatricians today ask mothers to have their children breathe into the telephone receiver.) Los Angeles is already planning emergency helicopter-lifted hospital units that go to the scene of an accident, drop the hospital pod, and then lift the wreckage out of the way so that traffic can resume.

As a total experiment in social science, human ecology, environmental biology, and environmental engineering, the

Experimental City would lend itself to a totally new concept of modern preventive medicine. Instead of healing the sick, doctors would contribute to the public-health concept that emphasizes the building up and banking of a capital of health and vigor while young, and the prudent spending of this capital over a lifetime without deficits of ill health. They would concentrate on eliminating ailments in early life rather than on repairing later ills. Their dedication, somewhat less personal in public health, would be, in a sense, what Dr. Walsh McDermott calls "statistical compassion."

Moreover, broad-band interconnections with other cities would provide smaller areas with wider access to national medical centers. Also, the educational, scientific, artistic, and entertainment opportunities would be far greater than a city of limited size would be able to offer otherwise. Point-to-point video, providing improved surveillance, should enable police to spend less time catching criminals after the event and more time preventing crimes.

Due to the present furor over the use of bugging and wire tapping, the information utility immediately invokes the specter of Big Brother and a Brave New World. In their best use, such devices can preserve and improve the quality of the urban environment, but like any other device they can also be misused by unscrupulous people. If the masses of information filed in our necessary public bureaus—the Internal Revenue Service, the National Institutes of Health, the Census Bureau, and the F.B.I.—were combined by an unscrupulous dictator, they would provide a potent coercive weapon against any individual. We cannot *not* use such devices, although we must set up adequate safeguards against their misuse. On the other hand, the information utility provides survey mechanisms for an instantaneous city census and flexible city management exactly analogous to methods of data collection used in weather forecasting.

The information utility and the mixing of living and working areas would reduce transportation needs, but it would still

be necessary to experiment with new forms of mass transportation. People like automobiles because the automobile
respects their desire to go directly from where they are to
where they want to be without stopping where others want
to stop. But the automobile produces polluting fumes and
occupies parking space when the owner is not in it—which is
about 90 per cent of the time.

Many suggestions have been made for a mass transportation system that retains the automobile's advantages without
incorporating its disadvantages. One such scheme calls for
pneumatically or electrically driven small pods with propul-
sion in the track. The pods may be computer-controlled to
the common destination of a few people. After indicating
your destination to the computer on entering the turnstile,
you would wait X minutes or until, let us say, the six-person
pod fills up—whichever is shorter—and then go nonstop to
your destination. The pods would be small enough to pass
noiselessly through buildings with normal ceiling heights.
There are no motors in the pods, and because they are inex-
pensive small shells, we could afford many of them.

In order for there to be no air-burning machines within the
city limits, connections to intercity and existing national
transportation systems might be made at the city's periphery.
Alternatively, airburning machines might come into the city
in underground tunnels with fume sewers. These would also
provide connections to the Experimental City's airport,
located at a distance and in a direction so that landing patterns are over not the city, but the noninhabited insulating
belt.

The main public utilities could be accessible in the vehicu-
lar and other underground tunnels, thereby abating the noisy
digging up and remaking of streets common to all American
cities. The interconnecting utility tunnels would double or
multiplex as traffic tunnels and utility trenches for the
transport of heavy freight, for telephone lines, for power and
gas lines, water and sewer mains, and for the rapid transit

of emergency vehicles—police, fire, and medical rescue. All would be below the city for increased mobility and less noise.

The sewers, with a view to conserving water, might be pneumatic as in the English and French systems. To save the immense areas occupied by present sewage-treatment plants, we might treat the sewage in transit in the sewer. All this presupposes that we can throw away the old-fashioned codes stipulating that telephone and power lines, and water mains and sewers be separate. Modern technology permits messages to be sent over power lines, and pure water pipes to be concentric with sewer mains. Just as garages can be housed under parks, all services can be underground, even to the extent of going hundreds of feet down for heavy manufacturing, storage of storm water, and snow and waste heat.

The Experimental City could also provide opportunities for test-marketing new products, building materials, and postal systems. New materials would give architects a tremendous scope in developing new forms. No traffic at ground level and no land owned by individuals or individual corporations would offer a degree of freedom not possible in cities where ownership of property delimits plots. Even the materials used in the buildings themselves would be such that they could be taken down and reused if found to be obsolete or inferior. Architecture, with its emphasis on form and the visual environment, is fundamental to the success of the Experimental City. Architects would be freer to exploit the mutuality of function and form in producing a visual environment *with* other improved qualities. In Philadelphia, for example, the planners have done a magnificent job improving the visual environment, but their work is mitigated by the stench of oil refineries.

In the Experimental City, we will seek a total optimum environment without hampering diversity of architectural forms and combinations. We will experiment with enclosing portions of the city within domes that will be conditioned as to temperature, humidity, fumes, and light. It is, of course, not at all certain that people want a perfectly controlled climate. The sense of beauty and well-being involves exposure to some degree of variation. Artists know this in their play with light and shade and with colors that clash. Slight breezes and variations of temperature might be necessary to transform even clean air into the fresh air that stimulates our sense of health.

The advantages of leasing and not owning land, combined with those of the new technologies, would free architects from rectilinear or stereotype ground plans that ownership of plots dictates. Space might be leased in a three-dimensional sense, and the forms the architects use in three dimensions might be emphasized by paths and foot thoroughfares, there being no wheeled traffic at ground level. Today, streets and plot plans too often predefine form. In the Experimental City, the architect will face the challenge of providing new ways for people to find face-to-face relationships in an environment that does not *require* wasteful movement.

Ralph Burgard has suggested that creative artists today are not so much concerned with the fixed audience-performer relationship. Many artists feel that art centers, now so much in fashion, are already outmoded, and that the newest forms of music, art, theater, and dance have very little to do with exhibit galleries, proscenium stages, and conventional auditoriums. Increased leisure should lead to active participation in all the arts instead of passive exposure. For this is needed an arts-recreation space completely flexible in lighting, sound, television, film, and electronic devices and in physical dimensions.

Where does one locate an Experimental City? It should be far enough away from urban areas so that it can develop self-sufficiency and not be hampered by the restrictive practices of a dominant neighboring community. Extremes of climate, far from being a disadvantage, would provide the kind of all-weather test facility needed for experimenting with technological innovations. There must be enough land for an insulating belt around the city; otherwise, conventional uncontrolled encroachments and developments would soon nullify the experiment. A density of one hundred people per acre in the city proper would mean a city area of 2,500 acres. To preserve its identity, character, cleanliness, and experimental freedom, it might need a hundred times this area as an insulating belt.

Federal and state governments are presently acquiring large tracts of unspoiled forests and lands for conservation. This is a worthy objective if done for some purpose. What better purpose is there than providing open space around cities? Such lands would be most suitable for the insulating belts between controlled-size, dispersed cities. The insulating belt would include forests, lakes, farms, outdoor museums, arboretums, and zoos. Such a mixture would make the enjoyment of the open surroundings not only attractive aesthetically and physically, but intellectually profitable. Part of the insulating belt might be devoted to hobby farms and gardens—the system so enjoyed by the Germans, who leave the city and camp in little gardens. This minimum rustic setting enables them to retain the smell and touch of the soil. There might also be high-intensity food farming and high-rise finishing farms. Fresh foods might be brought to farms in the insulating belt from starting farms farther out, and dairy cows could be fed in high-rise sterile buildings at the edge of the city to ensure the freshest, purest milk.

The legal codes and governmental structures of a city built with private funds on ground leased by a nonprofit corporation will be different from those of existing cities. Revenues to manage the city will come from leases rather than real-estate taxes. The laws and controls in the Experimental City will center on the new recognition of an individual's right to a clean environment. Though regulations will be different, there may be fewer of them because many of our laws evolved to protect us from the evil and nuisances precipitated by urban overgrowth. As the stresses of dirt, noise, and congestion are removed, other origins of antisocial behavior may be clarified.

Do people want dirt, noise, and congestion removed? Most of us assume so. But, like everything else in the Experimental City, we will have to see. The ideas and directions that have been suggested here are merely possible pieces of the total experiment, any one of which is likely to change and develop as the experiment itself develops.

About $330,000 have been allocated for defining the Experimental City project—three fourths from three departments of the Federal Government (Department of Commerce; Department of Health, Education, and Welfare; Department of Housing and Urban Development) and one fourth from local industries. This is to be used for surveys of literature and experience, conferences and workshops, and development of a structure for the program's next five phases. Laboratory evaluations of new concepts and systems will then be made and experimentation done with small-scale models. After a pilot model has been constructed so that a choice can be made among the various alternatives, the city will be designed, constructed, and occupied. Finally, the actual Experimental City will be studied further, changed, and developed.

The first year's work will be carried out with the University of Minnesota serving as the host and organizer of group discussions on a series of special topics. To these conferences we will invite interested national experts from many disciplines. A distinguished group of individuals has agreed to serve as a national steering committee for the Experimental City. After the year of definition, a suitable nonprofit corporation will be formed to carry through the later phases. Then a quasi-governmental, quasi-private corporation, following the experience of the Communications Satellite Corporation, will be formed to complete the building of the Experimental City and to oversee its subsequent operation.

Clearly, we cannot continue to experiment in bits: Each new technology affects others; better communications change patterns of travel, medical care, and education; methods of cleaning and noise-proofing make zoning unnecessary. The city is a completely interacting system, and, thus, the experiment must be a total system. Nobody knows the answers to city living in the future, and when answers are unknown, experiment is essential.

A lone planet
hurtling through space
encased in a narrow pocket of air
enriched with a few inches of fertile topsoil
endowed with a delicately cycled
flow of water . . .

Precariously balanced
at just the right distance from
and angle to the sun
rotating harmoniously
to alternate periods of light
and darkness
in proper porportion . . .

Such is the EARTH
with its marvelous conjunction
of intertwined elements
that make up
that incredible
combination of conditions
essential to human life.

How fragile
unreal
impossible
it all seems
when viewed
from
the astronaut's perspective.

The startling truth
is that this delicate globe
is manned!

It has
the beautiful
complex equipment
necessary
for man
to live
breathe
work
love
and pray.
Today Earth is in trouble.
The splendid balance
is gravely threatened.

All of man's
intelligence
imagination
and dedication
will have
to be roused
and fused
into a massive emergency operation
if we are
to demonstrate
our gratitude to
the Creator,
our concern
for the work of His hands,
and our concrete practical love
for each other.

James J. Megivern

Section Sources

CULTURAL BACKGROUND

Walter Orr Roberts, "Science, A Wellspring of Our Discontent," Sigma Xi–Phi Beta Kappa address at the meeting of the American Association for the Advancement of Science in Washington, D.C., on 29 December 1966. By permission of the author.　　　　　　　　　　　　　　　**p. 2.**

McCabe Pioneer Methodist Church, McMinnville, Oregon. Photo by John A. Day.　　　　　　　　　　　　**p. 3.**

"The Cultural Basis for Our Environmental Crisis," Moncrief, L. W., *Science*, Vol. 170, pp. 508-512, 30 October 1970. Copyright 1970 by the American Association for the Advancement of Science.　　　　　　　　　　　**p. 4.**

Walt Whitman, *Song of Myself.*　　　　　　　　**p. 18.**

Autumn, Knole House, near Sevenoaks, Kent, England. Photo by John A. Day.　　　　　　　　　　　　　**p. 19.**

"The Population Explosion and the Rights of the Subhuman World," John B. Cobb, Jr., School of Theology at Claremont, California.　　　　　　　　　　　　　　　**p. 20.**

Kaiser News, *Ecology: The Man-Made Planet.* Copyright 1970 by Kaiser Aluminum & Chemical Corporation.　**p. 34.**

Lisa. Photo by John A. Day.　　　　　　　　　**p. 35.**

"Our Treatment of the Environment in Ideal and Actuality," Yi-Fu Tuan, reprinted by permission from *American Scientist*, Vol. 58, pp. 244-249, May-June 1970.　　　**p. 36.**

GLOBAL ASPECT

John Donne, *Meditation XVII.* **p. 48.**

Jungfrau, Bernese Oberland, Switzerland. Photo by Frederic F. Fost. **p. 49.**

"Mortgaging the Old Homestead," Lord Ritchie-Calder, reprinted by permission of *Foreign Affairs,* January 1970. Copyright 1970 by the Council on Foreign Relations, Inc., New York. **p. 50.**

Gerard Piel, *The Computer as Sorcerer's Apprentice.* **p. 68.**

The Forest. Photo by John A. Day. **p. 69.**

"The Convergence of Environmental Disruption," Goldman, M. I., *Science,* Vol. 170, pp. 37-42, 2 October 1970. Copyright 1970 by the American Association for the Advancement of Science. **p. 70.**

KEY ELEMENTS: POPULATION AND ENERGY

William Vogt, *People.* **p. 90.**

Sister and Sleeping Brother, Tokyo, Japan. Photo by John A. Day. **p. 91.**

"Population and the Dignity of Man," Roger L. Shinn, an address delivered at The Consultation on the Identity and Dignity of Man, sponsored by The School of Theology of Boston University, with collaboration of Life Scientists on the Charles River Campus and the Medical Center and the American Association for the Advancement of Science, on 28 December 1969. Reprinted from *Identity and Dignity of Man,* ed. Preston Williams, Schenkman Publishing Company, Cambridge, Massachusetts (1971). **p. 92.**

Energy and Man: A Symposium. p. 110.

Transactions in Time. Copyright 1970, Kaiser Aluminum & Chemical Corporation. p. 110.

Log Fire. Photo by Peter Rose. p. 111.

"The Energy Revolution: Peril and Promise," George Taylor, *Man and His Environment,* AFL-CIO Publication No. 143, January 1969. p. 112.

BASIC APPROACHES TO THE SOLUTION

Orme Lewis, Jr. (Deputy Assistant Secretary, Public Land Management, U.S. Department of the Interior), a paper presented at the Council of Europe Conservation Conference in Strasbourg, France, in February 1970. p. 132.

Proteus, National Botanical Gardens, Cape Town, South Africa. Photo by Frederic F. Fost. p. 132.

"Ecosystem Science as a Point of Synthesis," S. Dillon Ripley and Helmut K. Buechner, reprinted by permission from *Daedalus,* Journal of the American Academy of Arts and Sciences, Vol. 96, No. 4 (Fall 1967). p. 134.

New Wine, A Report of the Commission on the Danforth Study of Campus Ministries. p. 144.

Contemplation, Page, Arizona. Photo by Peter Rose. p. 145.

"How Should the University Treat Environment?" (originally "How Should We Treat Environment?"), Hare, F. K., *Science,* Vol. 167, pp. 352-355, 23 January 1970. Copyright 1970 by the American Association for the Advancement of Science. p. 146.

Fisherman, City Park, Baton Rouge, Louisiana. Photo by Frederic F. Fost.   **p. 159.**

"From Conservation to Environmental Law," David Sive, reprinted by permission from *motive* magazine, April/May 1970.   **p. 160.**

Glen Canyon Dam, Page, Arizona. Photo by Peter Rose.
                                                            p. 169.

"Pollution Problems, Resource Policy, and the Scientist," Eipper, A. W., *Science,* Vol. 169, pp. 11-15, 3 July 1970. Copyright 1970 by the American Association for the Advancement of Science.   **p. 170.**

"The Next Industrial Revolution," Spilhaus, A., *Science,* Vol. 167, p. 1673, 27 March 1970. Copyright 1970 by the American Association for the Advancement of Science.   **p. 188.**

NCAR, National Center for Atmospheric Research, Boulder, Colorado. Photo by Peter Rose.   **p. 189.**

"The Experimental City," Athelstan Spilhaus, reprinted by permission from *Daedalus,* Journal of the American Academy of Arts and Sciences, Vol. 96, No. 4 (Fall 1967).   **p. 190.**

James J. Megivern, *God's Good Earth and Ours,* Courtesy of The Christophers, New York.   **p. 206-207.**

DATE DUE